The Law and Politics of Inclusion

On the one hand, inclusion constitutes a powerful framework of political agency, as people can gain access to forms of recognition granting legal protection and social visibility. On the other hand, inclusion requires their adherence to fixed matrices incorporating specific and limited forms of life. This opposition reflects a similar division within the academic field: between liberal advocates of inclusion and those who regard it as a form of assimilation, where differences are absorbed and tempered.

Uncovering the deficiencies in both viewpoints, this book analyzes inclusion by attending to the active role of subjects looking for inclusion, and mobilizing inclusive processes. Inclusion is thus reconceived as an ongoing, engaging movement of category-production, according to which there is no straightforward opposition between effective inclusion and assimilation. The book thus draws the idea of inclusion out of this opposition in order to delineate a form of political connectedness based on smaller social networks of solidarity that, although entailing some sort of normativity, are nevertheless characterized by fluidity and proximity. In this way, inclusion comes to be more productively, and more plausibly, reframed: as a web in which inclusive processes appear as moments of the renegotiation and rearticulation of a subjectivity in constant flux.

Valeria Venditti is a Postdoctoral Fellow in Political Philosophy at the University College Cork. Her research revolves around the issues of legal inclusion and political engagement. She got her Ph.D. at Sapienza, University of Rome and carried out her research in collaboration with Universiteit Antwerpen, Glasgow University and Charles University in Prague.

The Law and Politics of Inclusion

From Rights to Practices of Disidentification

Valeria Venditti

Routledge
Taylor & Francis Group
a GlassHouse Book

First published 2019
by Routledge
2 Park Square, Milton Park, Abingdon, Oxon OX14 4RN

and by Routledge
52 Vanderbilt Avenue, New York, NY 10017

First issued in paperback 2020

a GlassHouse book

Routledge is an imprint of the Taylor & Francis Group, an informa business

British Library Cataloguing-in-Publication Data
A catalogue record for this book is available from the British Library

Library of Congress Cataloging-in-Publication Data
A catalog record has been requested for this book

ISBN 13: 978-0-367-67107-5 (pbk)
ISBN 13: 978-0-8153-5657-8 (hbk)

Typeset in Galliard
by codeMantra

Contents

Acknowledgments

This book started life as a Ph.D. project on unspeakability and marginalization. Its pages are a sort of time travel into reflections and ideas that led me to discover new paths and imagine alternative ways to think of politics and its corollaries, to inhabit the social space and to take part in everyday exchanges.

I want to thank Colin Perrin and Nicola Sharpe, who kindly (and patiently!) followed me in the production of this text.

Writing this book would have not been possible without the guidance of my mentors and the support of friends and colleagues. I express all my gratitude to Vittorio Bufacchi, who believed in me and my project and offered me a fresh start, a new beginning in the academia. Always kind and attentive, he welcomed me and made me feel at home in a brand-new life. I owe a great debt to Virginio Marzocchi, who, notwithstanding our theoretical differences and my idiosyncrasies, sustained me with grace and strength during my whole academic career. Thanks to Caterina Botti, who initiated me to the academic life and allowed me to actively take part in her classes and seminars. Thanks to scholars and friends who taught me many things: Piergiorgio Donatelli, Olivia Guaraldo, George Pavlakos, Frederik Swennen. Thanks to my colleagues and friends who have inspired my thinking, answered my calls for help and discussed ideas and questions: Peter Agha, Lorenzo Bernini, Michele Spanò, Vincenzo Rosito, Francesca Tullii and her sparkling mind. Special thanks go to Marco Goldoni, valuable ally and sweet companion, and to Andrea Salvatore with his enigmatic, steady presence in my life, inside and outside the academia.

The development of this book has benefited from the generosity, time and love of many people. Laura, Vincenzo and Maria Laura who still put up with me. My brother Lorenzo, an irreplaceable figure in my life, who keeps teaching me many and many things. Rita, Anna and Valter who cooked a lot, sent me letters, sang Chinese songs on the beach, told me stories about their adventurous lives and give me lots of love. My cousins Ludovica and Giorgia, old souls under the guise of young girls in flower. My friends since ever Giorgia, Federica, Valentina, Fabio and Fabio. Thanks to Arianna, Enrica and Giulia, Margherita and Sara whose presence brightens up my days.

Thanks to Mariano, a great mentor, a lover, a friend, an inspiring scholar, an amazing teacher, a special reader, a tidy housemate, a glass of natural wine, an entry point, a whimsical point of view, a mismatch, a matchstick, a madrigal, a noise, a pointed nose, a corn can, a fold, a boon, a brown spot, a poem, a trip to Cilento, a walk on the grass, a statue in the Middelheim, an éclair, an éclat, a vibration, an endless desire. A life.

This work was supported by the Irish Research Council, Post-doctoral Fellowship Project-ID GOIPD/2018/360.

Introduction

The (incorpo)reality of inclusion

Social change happens regularly, on a daily basis, but changes can hardly be taken at face value. In particular, one can hardly measure the progressive or conservative character of change against the institutional texts or dynamics that bring it about. There is something that cannot be discovered in them, something that tends to be left unspoken. The thrust of this work is how the language of institutions allows for the articulation of forms of life and how certain forms are articulated to the disadvantage of others. This kind of question cannot be tackled in the abstract, for it requires alertness and sensitivity to historical and social processes that do not lend themselves to easy observation. Indeed, the type of approach that is necessary to undertake this study requires "a critical break with primary self-evidences", which is meant to "neutralize the effects of naturalization" (Bourdieu 1998:182). The historic lens that this work adopts is the specific, circumstantial relation between the political and the legal spheres, one that has been changing significantly since the 1990s. My main claim will be that, today's specific relation between law and politics, as well as the transformations that are affecting both policy frameworks and legal measures ignite mechanisms of social semantics whereby inclusion is turned into assimilation. A related claim will be that assimilation takes a specific shape in light of which the institutional language granting legal speakability (that is, a situation in which a given entity or problem can be accounted for with recourse to the official language of the law) requires forms of life to conform to it in order for them to be verbalized and then to exert effects of reality on the institutional semantics. As I will extensively discuss, the particular way in which the law works in today's societies of the Global North turns forms of inclusion into wide mechanisms of naturalization operating through narrow and reified categories of different types.

The range of institutional dynamics that I will look at comprises different sorts of inclusive policies. I decided to deal with the issue of inclusion because it is one of the prime instruments of democratic politics by which governments try to extend the range of people involved in ordinary politics. An issue that will emerge, although it will not be the focus of this work, is that inclusion today does not come in its traditional guise (civil society engagement, participation in public debates, contested elections) but morphs into the legal recognition of well-defined strands of the population characterized as groups in the light of institutionalized categories that are meant to define them as groups (ethnic populations, homosexuals, elders, women, transsexual people, people with disability, refugees, prostitutes). To this purpose, I will single out and examine three prototypical inclusive policies: ***opportunity-oriented***, ***capability-based*** and ***category-protecting*** ones. Later on, in this section, I will provide some details on how I put them to the test. For now, what I want to emphasize is the type of naturalized categories that they enact and revolve around: the citizen, the human being, the identity-based self. Needless to say, the way they deploy this naturalized core differs in light of the different nature of these policies. By the same token, it might be as easy to identify the functioning of specific categories in one model as it might be difficult to track it down in another. And yet, it is my contention that all of them set in motion the same basic movement whereby subjects and groups are, whether overtly or covertly, prompted to adapt themselves to a categorial platform. In other words, inclusion ceases to be a mode of enhancing political engagement and expanding and enriching active political participation. Rather, it takes the form of an "equalizer", a tool that smooths differences through the endowment of privileges and entitlements under the form of rights. Despite encouraging a kind of formal equality, this approach not only fragments society (nurturing the proliferation of identity groups and lobbies) and impoverishes general political participation. It also promotes standards of living by way of a legal recognition and prompts people to embrace these standards. Inclusion, in these terms, invokes conformation to a norm. It is no longer a question of participation: it is a call to homogenization.

However, the idea of inclusion turning into assimilation cannot be taken as a universal and trans-historical feature of Western democracies, for it is a transient element hallmarked by a particular history and resting upon a context-specific relationship between the spheres of law and politics. To point out the main features of this relation, it is imperative to detail some of the main changes that are occurring in these spheres.

Inclusion (and marginalization, its counterpart) has always represented a key element to think democratic institutions. However, in the second half of the 20th century a great transformation of its political value occurred. Phenomena such as economic growth and industrialization, geopolitical changes, and, above all, the emergence of transversal social entities transcending class and nationality (such as feminist and LGBT activism) as well as the upsurge of anti-racist, postcolonial, civil rights movements encouraged the expansion of a lively debate around social marginalization and how to deal with the challenge its new form represented. Discrimination appears to be a discrepancy between political opportunities offered to citizens and social participation granted to some of them. While, in principle, every citizen can take part in democratic processes and institutions, some people's life is marked by a form of subtle discrimination that permeates everyday experience and hampers the possibility of being politically active. Marginalization takes the form of a poor neighbourhood, of a low-paid job, the impossibility of accessing social privileges, the denial of civic rights. In this sense, political upsurges that characterized the end of the 20th century shed light on the uneven fabric of which nation states are made. Henceforward, in Western democratic societies, inclusion started to be directed to subjects as elements of discrete categories. The "Citizen" began to appear as a kind of awkward political exception: the bearer of *universal* rights that are precluded to many of those with whom *he* shares a territory, a constitution, a government. From black people, to women, from lesbians and gays to people with disability, there was a crowd showing that "We, the people" were quite a small bunch of persons in the heterogeneous horde that populate the nation state.

So: what does political inclusion mean *actually*? How is it possible for Western democracies to fail to notice the vast range of discrimination that affects their acolytes? And, how to *promote* a form of radical inclusion in democratic regimes? How to defeat, once and for all, social marginalization, in order to establish a *fairer* society?

In the following pages, I will provide a brief theoretical detour on inclusion and sketch out an account of contemporary inclusive strategies. This will introduce the reader to the basic insights of this book. The first one is that our political experience of inclusion boils down to the creation of top-down legal forms of recognition, which reduces inclusion to a *procedure* rather than a *process*; to an act of *befitting* rather than one of *becoming*. The result is a juridification of inclusion and a general limitation of its political potential.[1] The second one is that this form of inclusion is a contradiction in terms: on the one hand, it requires an "outside" to define its boundaries. On the other hand, it operates through the creation of grids of intelligibility *actively* banishing some realities while recognizing certain forms of life. Legal inclusion, in fact, obliterates some ways of living by legitimizing specific ways of embodying and embracing determinate identities and categories. The outcomes of this attitude will constitute the core of this work.

Inclusion has come to be seen by many, and by specific schools of thought, as the landmark of democracy (see e.g. Habermas 2005; Rawls 1971; Sen 2010; Young 1990, 2000). One of the basic assumptions that underlie the connection between democracy and inclusion is that inclusion is bound up with the legitimation of political procedures and of society's juridico-political structure as a whole, for "political outcomes can only be legitimate if those who must abide by or adjust to them have had a part in their formation" (Young 2000:53). Democratic polities have the duty to stay sensitive to citizens' demands and to listen to the broadest possible segment of the population. In this sense, a high degree of participation allows the recognition of different levels and facets of civil society, as well as the recognition of its constitutive plurality. To put it another way, such recognition enables a bidirectional form of public engagement, in which every voice can potentially be heard, and every experience

1 For a focus on juridification, see Croce (2018). With "political potential", as I will explain in due course, I refer to the openness of any social process that takes form, develops and changes *within* social relationships. This process is at odds with any juridified procedure, in which both the terms and the conditions of a phenomena are given. The political potential explodes in the ongoing, unpredictable unfolding of events (see e.g. Deleuze 2004).

can potentially be voiced. Within this framework, the legitimation of political authority consists both in trying to address the broadest range of situations and in guaranteeing representation for most of the citizens.

However, while the pursuit of inclusion might be a democracy stock-in-trade, the way in which liberal states of the Global North address marginalization in these days is of a very specific kind. The most effective political strategy to defeat marginalization appears to involve the extension of political and civic rights and/or the provision of legal protection to discriminated social elements. In spite of the growing number of policymakers and scholars who have dealt with the issue of inclusion, marginalization and social justice, there is no agreed-upon criterion on how to include, whom to include and the modes of inclusion. Nonetheless, political and social movements of the 60s and 70s opened up a new perspective on the value of inclusion. To be politically recognized and to have the opportunity to participate and take action within democratic institutions cannot be reduced to political enfranchisement but has to start with a broader process of social legitimation. A process that involves the public recognition of a whole private sphere in which personal conducts and identities are shaped. From this point of view, inclusion should be considered the engine of a democratic approach that cares for people's lives *beyond* their institutional weight. This fresh look on inclusion is rooted in the idea that a person comes to be constituted by the cluster of discursive, affective, power relations that compose her environment and that the state is but one of the systems to which she belongs. Social movements based on identity (such as feminism) shed a light on the multiplicity of belongings that characterizes any life. In this sense, the acknowledgement of what was beyond the public side of a citizen's life came to be considered as a basic feature of political inclusion. By following this inclination, an inclusive democracy should develop into a political platform that welcomes diversity as a pillar of political processes and institutional functionings. Political participation should sprout from the public recognition of different existing practices and ways of living. Through inclusion, democratic states honour the promise of a public space keen on differences, in which a plurality of life forms find their place.

Still, the proliferation of alternative forms of life in a democratic society does not represent just a value in itself. It acquires significance in relation to the main features that marginalization retains. As Iris Marion Young (1990:48–63) has observed, marginalization appears as a multilayered condition which often emerges in the conjunction of different circumstances. The presence (or co-presence) of conditions such as oppression, powerlessness, violence and cultural imperialism creates a state of social seclusion. It is possible to notice, in fact, that marginalization and discrimination emerge out of the concurrence of elements that mostly concern the private side of a subject's life. Before being excluded from the possibility of exercising political rights, marginalized people are prevented from participating in a wide range of social exchanges.[2] Marginalization

2 On this, see Secchi and Viganò (2009) and Secchi (2013).

takes a concrete form, one that affects the subjects themselves, instead of being attached to the space they inhabit. Marginalization turns into a corporeal attribute, a real attitude: it becomes *a matter of identity.* Marginalized subjects find themselves in a secluded state of idle powerlessness, that is, a state in which single individuals are no longer able to operate in accordance with their goals, nor improve their conditions. They find themselves deprived of means, both material and cognitive (see e.g. Fricker 2006; Langton 1993) and suffer from a lack of connections and interactions. This condition marked by separateness hampers the possibilities of finding appropriate solutions to one's own condition and contributes to enhance the gap between marginalized individuals and their surrounding reality (see Bauman 2004). The inward collapse of spatial boundaries (the turning of a person into its own borders – see Sossi 2006) is accompanied by a simultaneous alteration of the experience of time. Marginalization not only means to survive in the interstices of the social realm, but also to be caught up in a frantic rhythm, in which necessity saturates the horizon of a lifetime (Mullainathan and Shafir 2013), dividing it "into episodes, each one cut from its past and from its future, each one self-enclosed and self-contained" (Bauman 1996:10). Under this light, marginalization reveals itself as a circular, self-nurturing condition, since "no consistent and cohesive life strategy emerges from the experience which can be gathered in such a world" (Bauman 1996:10).

In addition, it must be observed that what determines marginalization, delineating single individuals' social position and their ability to take action within the social realm (both at a political and at a personal level), originates far beyond the finite time and space of a life. Single instances of marginalization take roots in an extrinsic, sedimented general discourse. Exclusion is the result of the naturalization and universalization of specific cultural patterns, tightly connected with habits and traditions of dominant groups. The imposition of a *signifying regime* hampers the "hybridization" (Donlan 2012; Menski 2014) of practices and the multiplication of instruments to interpret and regulate them. The universalization of a specific cultural matrix brings about a dichotomy between a well-defined group, which embodies the model for all social and legal norms, and a cohort of heterogeneous subjectivities, generally marked in negative terms: an-other who is *no(t-the)one.* By universalizing clusters of principles set in narrations, what happens to become the hegemonic group fosters a rhetoric of naturalism and determinism and delineates a finite number of possible identities and viable relations. Nonetheless, what looks like a saturating matrix cannot but be contingent on the group of "others" that it obliterates. In fact, it is precisely in the emergence of a generic difference that a system of "cultural imperialism" can be instantiated. Still, the recognition of an essential gap between "we" and the "others" proves instrumental in maintaining subordination, as the latter emerges as a shapeless territory, a "dark continent"[3] which cannot be

3 I use this expression in relation to Luce Irigaray's (1974) mordacious comments on the role of femininity in the history of occidental thought.

identified and often lacks the instruments for articulating its experience of the social world. In this context, the others become the "logical operators in [the] discursive production" of "a tightly constructed system that requires difference as pejoration in order to erect the positivity of the norm" (Braidotti 1994:80). By failing to fulfil normative standards, "the others" define the borders of social acceptability, with their presence, their bodies, their conducts. For this reason, marginalization "involves the paradox of experiencing oneself as invisible at the same time that one is marked out as different" (Young 1990:60). Nonconforming, marginalized and discriminated people, categories and groups are read and read themselves through the lenses of *a* hegemonic grid of sense and cannot but rely on the dominant system to seek intelligibility. The difficulty to express nonconventional desires, attitudes and relational bonds through referring to a determinate "signifying chain" (Deleuze and Guattari 1987:112) redoubles marginalization as something that silences nonconventional experiences while casting light on them. In addition to entailing a limited access to certain practices and domains of the social realm, social exclusion implicates the subtle erosion of linguistic formulae to poignantly articulate one's own condition. It sets in motion, a movement of disqualification of alternative social realities. The displacement of unconventional narrations results from the fact that a discursive account of nonconforming conditions still depends on a set of meanings which tends to convey a norm, forcing the infinite variations of human living in a finite number of variables. A language still relying on a map of the ordinary, that marks someone as an unintelligible outsider.

The twofold grip that I have described so far (the personal loss of space and time and the impossibility of accounting for one's own condition) affects subjects both as single individuals and as members of a group, whose identity and social position can hardly be articulated within the hegemonic signifying regime. Here lies the problem with marginalization: in being determined by a concurrence of different factors, a political resolution that tackles only the most visible aspect of its occurrence is bound to fail. If only because such factors lead inevitably to an expansion of the private sphere, at the expense of the participation to the public one. To constitute one's own border equates to be relegated in the here and now of myopic connections and in the painstaking succession of voiceless experiences. This gives life to an unbridgeable gap among marginalized subjects and what surrounds them. The twofold (cultural and personal; enacted and experienced) banishment to which they are exposed can be identified as both the outcome and the source of marginalization.

Indeed, to participate in the public debate and in basic democratic political procedures appears as an important resource to defeat discrimination. If democracy is conceived as constitutively structured on (active and/or passive) participation to institutional procedure, the difficulty in taking part in basic political exchanges and having an active role in the public debate emerges indeed as a major problem. In this sense, the strong tie between democracy and inclusion might come out as mostly contingent on the recognition of an equal political weight of all the members of a democratic state. However, political inclusion represents a necessary but not sufficient solution to social exclusion. Marginalization requires an open understanding of the different modalities to treat its polymorphic instances. In this light, any legal approach aimed at defeating marginalization represents a tricky solution, since it anchors the process of inclusion to a univocal form of legitimation. Legal norms always have to outline and address specific subjects and circumstances (see Chapter 4). This means that they are bound to simplify – or at least cut to pieces – complex social elements to offer ready-made solution to well-recognizable and identifiable problematic situations. A legal norm is, by nature, steady and rigid and, thus, prone to articulate the question of inclusion as a linear one.[4]

Yet, the governmental technique that at present is designed to organize both institutions and subjects revolves around the endowment of legal instruments. In this scenario, the exercise of supreme sovereignty (typical, at least on paper, of modern statehood) is granted by the deployment of a governmental horizontal power premised upon a type of production of negotiation-based governmental tools (Spanò 2013).

This new way of instituting and regulating the social world takes the law as its primary means. The legal instrument replaces the deliberative and reflexive political organization on the part of a geohistorically circumscribed public power in order to foster an immanent and constantly *in fieri* politics, grounded on procedural actions administered at different levels by different social bodies. This managerial mechanism favors the proliferation of normative frameworks within which social actors have recourse to legal instruments to attain political effects. This movement can be epitomized as a withdrawal from, and a return to, the law. On the one hand, as law ceases to be the expression of a state-centred hierarchy, it undercuts the idea itself of public engagement as the linchpin of liberal-democratic regimes. On the other hand, law comes back under the form of a private weapon in the hands of social actors, who hold it in order to claim portions of power and define their space in the social realm. In this sense, the law largely becomes an adversarial device transforming courts and lawyers, rulings and sanctions into the elements of a *new political grammar*. The value of this fractalized dissemination of power can be measured against the multiplication of sources of power and the mobilization of forms of engagement alternative to traditional political ones. Despite this, the cultural value of the law declines, since such an engagement carried out through the means of the law does not result in an engagement capable of redefining the signifiers of the law itself (Merry 2006).

Law's character is at one and the same time enabling and subjugating. The acquisition of a political stance achieved through the deployment of the legal jargon always eventuates in the subjection to the very symbolic system that such a jargon incorporates. This emerging mode of representation allows social actors to gain a political profile, but in return, devalues traditional and

4 Many philosophers have analyzed, from different perspectives, the crystallizing patterns of legal recognition. Among the others, see Butler (1997b) and Deleuze (2004:19–21).

more orchestrated ways to articulate and revise the political sphere (Bourdieu 2004; see also Conclusion).

The hypothesis I just sketched to outline the fundamental leitmotiv of this text will be substantiated in the next chapters. Although I will not delve into the paradigm change that I summarized above, this will be both a basic premise of my discussion and something that I will vindicate as we go along. My discursive strategy will be to identify three dominant models of enabling people to engage with institutions and to obtain political effects that are supposed to ameliorate their life conditions. These models are at one and the same time, distinct from each other and profoundly similar to one another. In order for me to claim that they are similar, however, I will need to pinpoint what makes them different. A shared fundamental trait is the hypostatization of an imagined addressee of their policies, and yet, when we look at the addressee that lies at their core, it might seem untenable to liken them. However, a deeper exploration into each of them will show that they are not as much similar when it comes to the substance of this addressee as they are when it comes to the mechanism deployed for concealing the very presence of a hypostatized addressee. In other words, these models put in place a form of concealment that allows them to glue together inclusion and progressiveness and to claim that the two are synonyms; but what they all disguise is a basic premise that they all neglect: the need to posit, but at the same time, systematically ignore, an unstated subject.

The first type of policy approach I will discuss in Chapter 1, the opportunity-oriented approach, assumes political participation to be the best way to prompt people to play an active part in everyday politics. This strategy is meant to address individuals as citizens, that is, as public actors, from which will follow the necessary delineation and constitution of a public sphere as completely separate and detached from the private one. My claim will be that the very perpetration of a disentanglement between the private and the public, which is alleged to empower the subject as a citizen, ratifies naturalized divisions of roles and hierarchies in the private sphere, as policies of this sort pay exclusive heed to the political-public sphere and remain blind to those (private) differences that are the primary source of discrimination and marginalization. As a paradigmatic case, I will examine feminist scholars' concerns about the private/public divide. By drawing on Catherine MacKinnon (e.g. 1987, 2006), Sally Haslanger (e.g. 2012), Rae Langton (e.g. 1993) and Iris Marion Young (e.g. 1997), I will contend that the elision of the private as a fundamental tool to instantiate the artificial construction of the public citizen makes opportunity-oriented strategies fall short. Even worse, it creates the condition for the maintenance of existing social hierarchies and disadvantages insofar as the public display of good intentions on the part of state institutions belittles the need to cut deeper into the subtlest causes of inequalities that are based on "private" deficiencies (which I will describe as a threefold lack of horizon, terms and power).

The second type of policies, the capability-based approach, seems to enact a very different – if not opposite – kind of strategy. The emphasis here is placed on people's private life, something which inheres in people's basic and potential skills to attain an actual and effective political participation. Apparently then, these policies work as a felicitous correction of the first strategy. The advocates of these models, in particular Martha Nussbaum and Amartya Sen, offer a theoretical structure that aims at indicating where and when state institutions should intervene to redress circumstances of marginalization and discrimination. For them, the key to liberal inclusion comes to be very much linked to individual's actual needs and inclinations. My argument against this perspective will read that for the supporters of this policy model to identify spheres of intervention, they need to postulate, whether explicitly or implicitly, the existence of a basic human nature. Such a paradigm is known well enough for me not to describe it further (albeit a deepest scrutiny is offered in Chapter 2) to indicate directly which are the main flaws of this approach. As I will discuss by building on the work of scholars in Disability Studies – such as Tom Shakespeare (2006) and Michael Berubè (1996) – and Crip Theory – such as Robert McRuer (2006) and Allison Kafer (2013) – the production of an allegedly homogeneous humanity not only banishes physical aspects of marginalization but constitutes some realities as permanently and inescapably inhuman. The examples of policies that seek to promote the integration of people with disabilities reveal the tendency to implement activities that could help those people to cope with the neutral environments and structures of everyday society. The burden of inclusion (that is, of being included, of proving capable of being included) falls entirely on the impaired subject, denying the role of an organization (material, socio-spatial and temporal) structured around (and for) healthy and able-bodied individuals. As I will argue, this is but an example of the way in which some political and theoretical paradigms tend to take for granted, widespread features of a majority of the population as hallmarks of a shared humanity, which therefore work as a threshold and as a system of measurement.

The account of the third approach, i.e., category-protecting policies, will be a major step to the discovery of the similarities among the three models. In effect, this type of policy seems far away from the latter two because of an explicit categorial filter, which is set in motion for them to address specific policy targets. And yet, I will contend that this way of functioning is archetypal and can be observed as being at work in the latter two models when we look at them not only as policies, but as alternative systems that contribute to the production of a substantive and formative symbolic core. In this sense, analyzing the third type of policies will be key to understanding how, by claiming to be redeeming the situation of marginalized subjects, policies at the same time constitute these subjects, or better contribute to the semantic construction of the social situation in which they claim to be. In short, the exploration of category-protecting policies will lead me to elucidate how policy measures construct and introduce categories to address someone as a member of a group (e.g., as gay or lesbian, gipsy, potential terrorist or prostitute), and by doing so, postulate the existence of a basic link between one's belonging to a social group and some traits that are claimed to qualify their identity as social beings. Subjects are taken to be members of categories that the law not only legitimates but constructs to make these people legally speakable.

The scrutiny and the implicit juxtaposition of the three types of policies will lead me to identify, the main traits of today's mechanism of speakability-conferring systems. In particular, it will be my claim that the three types of policies exemplify the typical movement whereby the inclusion of people and the portrayal of situations of marginalization are mediated by categories that group people together and, precisely by doing so, inadvertently naturalize these groups as basic components of society. Chapter 4 will contend that today's upsurge of rights, as the main political device for people to claim political recognition and to exert political effects, is redolent of this mechanism of social semantics. I will explain that the notion of rights is particularly nuanced and cannot be taken as a stable signifier throughout history. On the contrary, rights follow the trajectory (that I summarized above) by which law is, on the one hand, withdrawing, and, on the other hand, coming back as a powerful political device in the hands of individuals. Accordingly, in stark contrast to former types of rights, today's rights (what I will call "millennial rights") celebrate the disjunction between the political, shared organization of society, attained through an orchestrated and committed engagement, and the recognition of segmented strands of the population that are granted legal protection because of inward-looking, by and large apolitical reasons and because of these strands being regarded as homogeneous social entities. In this way, at present we are witnessing a major fracture between rights as a pre-state, pre-political, pre-legal element characterizing human beings and the level where the law is deliberately employed and deployed to design and enact a joint political project.

Chapter 5 will get to the core of the mechanism of the production of categories that the former chapters will indirectly discuss to set forth a theoretical view mainly based on the notion of "looping effect". By this analysis, I will aim to foreground the relationship – fundamental to present day rights – between inclusion and the classification of the recognized segments of society. The looping effect (Hacking 1995a, 1995b, 1999) is by no means a distinguishing mark of the law alone, given that the performative force of classification is a permanent feature of all classificatory endeavours, especially as far as the social world and its components are concerned. Nonetheless, I will make the point that the shift which is affecting the legal tool at present transforms it in such a way that the law favours the production of classifications, which in their turn are embraced by social actors who identify themselves with the offered categories. In this scenario, I will insist on these mechanisms being a feedback loop. It is neither the law which imposes classification, nor the subject who endorses them; rather, it is the conjunction between the two movements, or better, the interaction between categories serving as frames for self-understanding and these categories being used as recognition-conferring instruments. Therefore, the legal tool is not used to erode classifications, as it tends more and more to endorse and to ratify them as though they were affixed to nature and hence outside the flux of history (Haslanger 2006).

Chapter 6 will finally constitute the constructive side of this work. It will first cast light on the political relevance of the transformations that are affecting the legal technique with particular attention to the instrument of rights. One of my main concerns will be to show how and why the three types of policies that I discuss in the first part of this work share the type of categorization that I examine in Chapter 5. Then, by drawing on Davina Cooper's (2004) distinctions between direct governing, mid-way governing and governing at a distance, I will single out the type of governing techniques that these three models set in motion. By doing so, I will explain how the relationship between politics, law and language ceases to be the context of an ongoing revision and an incessant discovery. To this end, I will introduce the notion of "governance of governance", that is, the key governmental instrument whereby institutions mould and handle the basic format for legal recognition.

Based on this critical analysis, this work will conclude by advocating not so much a different understanding of politics, but instead a different understanding of the sources of critical and symbolic forces that might allow revising and redressing those situations that, in my opinion, are the main factors behind marginalization and exclusion. In effect, given the existing conditions of politics and law both at a local and a global level, it would be naive to make the case for a renewed strong politics that might re-establish a deep link between politics as a sphere where the social can be jointly imagined and modelled, and law as the sphere where these results are implemented, tested, verified and revised. This, however, does not mean that the only option is bid farewell to the very idea of politics as the construction of alternatives. By building on Cooper's (2013) visions of utopian politics as a micropolitical project, where the actual conditions of present politics are imagined in such a way that transformative effects might be actively anticipated, I will argue for a valuation of minorstream contexts where alternatives are not simply fantasized about but concretely operated despite failures and perhaps even in light of failures.

1 Model 1

Opportunity-oriented policies

The first model of inclusive policies I will analyze works on the assumption that increasing participation and political enfranchisement are the best ways to tackle social and political marginalization. This approach is meant to prompt people to play an active part within political institutions, for participation is taken as an inherent mark of an equalitarian democracy and public engagement is claimed to prevent the formation of enclaves of marginalization. While the former allows gathering different voices from disparate positions within society and giving them political visibility; the latter grants every citizen (without any distinction based on "personal features" such as sex, class, colour, religion) to access to the public forum, as well as the possibility of expressing their interests and affecting political decisions, especially through procedural mechanisms (such as vote).

Thus, as the name suggests, opportunity-oriented strategies mainly aim at offering to every citizen the *opportunity* to take part in decisional processes and democratic procedures. To do so, strategies and norms based on this model are concerned with regulating the public aspects of people's life. In this sense, inclusion is considered to follow from *equality* and is articulated as a formal achievement. Inclusion and equality are understood as two necessary features of social justice. Yet, social justice (as I will show in this chapter) appears here as a very narrow concept. Opportunity-oriented policies limit their consideration of social justice to the public, shared, political space and conceive it as "the absence of social injustice" (Bufacchi 2012:1). Legal interventions and political strategies against marginalization are organized with a view on obtaining a fair arrangement of society. A democracy in which every subject counts as a citizen, that is, as *a member* of the polity endowed with all the rights and tasks of *all the other members*. Marginalization, in this approach, can be defeated through reclaiming a linear, logical political premise: equality makes equals.

Still, the price to treat everybody as equal, as equally included and *able* to join political life as a member of a political community, fails to weigh up the *reasons behind* marginalization. Opportunity-oriented strategies, to say it with Judith Shklar (in Bufacchi 2012:3), take "for granted that injustice is simply the absence of justice, and that once we know what is just, we know all we need to know". The notion of political visibility and participation as a means to defeat marginalization "misses a great deal". Shklar hits the mark, when she observes:

> The sense of injustice, the difficulties of identifying both the unjust person and the victims of injustice, and the many ways in which we all learn to live with each other's injustices tend to be ignored, ***as does the relation of private injustice to public order.*** (Shklar in Bufacchi 2012:3, emphasis added)

In this model, social justice is pursued by considering only the public, ignoring its relation to the private sphere. Inclusion and equality are thus two aims to be achieved through the constitution of a "safe zone", where individual traits and personal choices (that could feed prejudiced behaviours or unfair interactions) are banished. All citizens ***are made*** equal in front of the law. They have a place in the polity, no matter what their private, pre-political experience is.

While this blindness to the non-public side of citizens' lives might retain positive results in granting a formal participation to proceduralized tasks in a democratic regime, this model ends up considering only those forms of discrimination that present a public aspect. In this chapter, I will argue that beneath the rhetoric of political equality and public inclusion, opportunity-oriented strategies tend to establish and reinforce an exclusionary system and are unable to modify, change or even challenge the traditional system of meaning or the social hierarchy that underlie and cause exclusion.

My argument will go as follows: I will begin by introducing an analysis of the outcomes of the private/public divide. Then, I will take as a case in point the trajectory of feminism. By looking at one of the foundational texts of liberal feminism,[1] *The Declaration of Sentiments*, I will illustrate how the interest of early feminists was in acquiring visibility in the political field in order to defeat a condition of discrimination that affected both their private and public positions. Liberation was the path to enjoy the same rights their male peers enjoyed. However, the core of their battles was not to be ***recognized*** as citizens, rather they aim at conquering a position in the social realm that could change their position in the private sphere. They wanted to be ***equal*** in front of the law, to make their way through an emancipated life. They asked for enfranchisement, education; they asked for a life for their own, for material liberation from masculine domination. No matter under what form (a job, a room, a voice in the Parliament), emancipation had to explode in the public arena, but its sparkles should light up an entire life. After that, I will gather things up and follow Catharine MacKinnon in a critical evaluation of all those political models that disregard the private sphere to refer only to an allegedly plain and linear public realm in which to create the equal conditions to foster inclusion. In this last section, I will not be concerned with putting to test MacKinnon's theories, ideas and style.[2] My interests in her work lies in her account of the unfair social

1 As I explain below, I will use the definition "liberal feminism" in a very narrow sense. With this locution, I will refer to a movement mainly interested to the public impact of feminism and to its political results.

2 Far more celebrated authors have taken issue with some flawed outcomes of MacKinnon's theoretical rigidity. It is impossible to provide an exhaustive list of the voices of the endless debate

system we live in. By harshly criticizing the most part of legal resolutions and political organization (always, in her view, detrimental for women), MacKinnon provides us with a zealous insight on what is the problem of marginalization and formal inclusion. In a nutshell, the problem lies in the sedimented hierarchy and unfair system that no resolution whatsoever can address *from within* the system. Once we use the political tools of an utterly manly state, no space can be created for what is different: the centre will always belong to those who have written the rules. Needless to say, MacKinnon's investigation concentrates on women's discrimination and subjection, however, I invite the reader to consider the argument raised for women as a discourse that can be generalized. Women are "the others" of those who created the state (allegedly white, adult, able men in Greece few centuries ago, or, at least, this is what Aristotle avers), but every centre has a periphery, every "One" has an "Other" to which he relates.

Opportunity-oriented policies promote a formal inclusion, realized through granting access to political procedures to every citizen. One of the main flaws of this approach concerns the ambiguous bifurcation of the concept of equality they inadvertently support. In being based on a division between a private and a public sphere, and in considering as politically meaningful only the latter, equality assumes at least two political weights. As Susan Moller Okin (1989) observes, the perpetration of such a division produces a fracture in the social realm grounded on the imposition of a naturalized division of roles and based on the recognition of a "normal", neutral, non-specific pole in relation to which other poles come to be identified (Okin 1989:93–94). It is in this binary structure that the model of the Citizen (the adult, able, respectable man) comes to be juxtaposed to an undefined group of "others", which might variously be identified as different because of their sex, gender, skin colour, ethnicity, religion and so on. The creation of a difference-blind political sphere neither flattens nor harmonizes divergences. Instead, it relegates the tensions they bring about in the private sphere, where primary causes of discrimination often originate and reproduce.

To understand the tricky results of this approach, it is worth looking into the case of sexual equality. Among the many instances that might depict the limits of this kind of policies, the issue of women and, more broadly, gender equality provides a perfect example, since it offers a historical perspective on the outcomes of this strategy on marginalized groups. The trajectory of feminism and the transformation of feminist's demands and struggles gives an account of the flaws inherent to a political recognition that leaves out an entire sphere of a citizen's life.

It is by now commonly acknowledged that "feminism" is composed of a relatively broad range of civic movements and covers a wide spectrum of questions concerning women, womanhood and oppression in general.[3] However, in the following pages, I will refer to an early instance of the feminist movement and

with and about MacKinnon here. In this chapter, I will refer to Wendy Brown (1989) and Judith Butler (1997b)'s works, but many others should be mentioned.

3 For an overall reading of the history of feminism and the differences among its different strands (see e.g. Cavarero and Restaino 2002; Freedman 2002; Walters 2006).

treat it as a cohesive one. This simplification is key to develop a linear analysis of the shift that led from a feminism mostly concerned with the acquisition of political enfranchisement, to one mainly oriented towards the recognition of the (political) centrality of private experiences (see, among many others, Crispin 2017; Friedan 1963; Lonzi 2010). My aim here is to illustrate that, even when primarily directed at gaining political visibility, feminist claims kept seeking a recognition that could relieve their private condition. In other words, it seems clear that, even in the most "political" inclined demands for recognition, feminists looked at formal political equality as a means to change the personal situation of women.[4]

The struggle for women's equality (organized and structured as a thick political movement) dates back to the end of the 18th century, when women began to ask for social visibility. In those days, exceptional "hyenas in a petticoat"[5] started a debate destined to grow quickly; the oppression to which women were exposed, they contended, was a cultural fact dependent on the organization of society and not on natural hierarchies. Women were segregated in a private dimension and did not have the possibility of publicly raising their voices in society. They lacked power, education and freedom, and, for these reasons, were trapped in a situation of vulnerability.

The famous *Declaration of Rights and Sentiment* (1848)[6] is exemplary. This document marks the beginning of a feminist movement that recognizes political enfranchisement as its main aim. The document, edited by Elizabeth Cady Stanton, Lucretia Mott and the group of activists gathered at the Seneca Falls Convention, identified some of the basic premises that underpin the challenges posed by the pursuit of sexual equality. Activists grounded their demands for equal rights in the assumption that every form of subordination takes place in a public framework and, thus, that any struggle for recognition should aim at unrooting the innate equality among men and women, overcoming a socially constructed and imposed hierarchy:

> We hold these truths to be self-evident: that all men and women are created equal; that they are endowed by their Creator with certain inalienable rights; that among these are life, liberty, and the pursuit of happiness; that to secure these rights governments are instituted, deriving their just powers from the consent of the governed. (Cady Stanton, Mott et al. 1848)

4 The passage from a feminism concerned with formal equality (the Suffragettes movement and their struggles for political enfranchisement) to a radical feminism struggling for a recognition of a substantial *difference* between men and women indicates precisely the maturation of the awareness that recognition cannot take the form of a plain annexation into an already made system.

5 "Hyena in a petticoat" is the label that Horace Walpole attributed to Mary Wollstonecraft. During the 18th century, voices like Wollstonecraft's were sporadic and uncommon. Women did not have the possibility of gathering in meetings and a "proper" movement – with massive political outcomes – emerged only during the 19th century. Yet, insulated theoretical and narrative experiences, brought about by single women or in little circles, were key to the creation of feminist thought and feminist movements.

6 The document, based on the United States Declaration of Independence, was mainly authored by Elizabeth Cady Stanton and was presented in 1848 at the Seneca Falls Convention. See http://ecssba.rutgers.edu/docs/seneca.html (last visited on 19 September 2018).

From this excerpt, it is possible to catch a glimpse of what would turn out to be the core of "liberal"[7] feminist battles in the years to come. The authors of the *Declaration* look remarkably aware of the system in which women were caught; they believe "[t]he history of mankind" to be "a history of repeated injuries and usurpations on the part of man toward woman, having in direct object the establishment of an absolute tyranny over her". Tyranny is described as the fact that rights "which are given to the most ignorant and degraded men – both natives and foreigners" such as rights of "citizen, the elective franchise, [...] the rights in property [...]" have been "withheld from [women]". If these sentences sound extremely ground-breaking, the perspective of the writers goes far more deeply, envisioning the crucial value of creation of two "spheres of action". They aver what follows:

> He [the man] has created a false public sentiment by giving to the world a different code of morals for men and women, by which moral delinquencies which exclude women from society, are not only tolerated, but deemed of little account in man.
>
> He has usurped the prerogative of Jehovah himself, claiming it as his right to assign for her a sphere of action [...]. He has endeavoured, in every way that he could, to destroy her confidence in her own powers, to lessen her self-respect, and to make her willing to lead a dependent and abject life. (Cady Stanton, Mott et al. 1848)

The *Declaration* provides a pithy description of how women were subordinated to men and at the same time, proposes and demands a specific solution: to give women political representation in order to release them from an imposed seclusion. This proposal is rooted in an overturning of the condition whereby women "if married" (but also if not) appeared, "in the eye of the law, civilly dead" (Cady Stanton, Mott et al. 1848).

The collective beyond the *Declaration* seeks, in the first place, a formal, institutional equality. The authors articulate their longing for emancipation as a request for accessing the public space. The recognition they strive to achieve moves from the entitlement to actively participate in the political debate to the incorporation into the legal body of problems and questions concerning women and their private life. For the supporters of the liberal paradigm, elective franchise, the possibility to actively participate in the public sphere, the inclusion of a certain issue in the political agenda is conducive not only to the demolition of the barriers that confine women in the domestic sphere, but also, and above all, to the liberation from a state of minority and subjugation.

7 Cavarero and Restaino (2002) use the term "liberal" to indicate those feminist movements aimed at providing women with political visibility. In common use, liberal feminism can either entail a position mainly centred on personal and political autonomy or refer more broadly to freedom as freedom from any form of coercion. Again, liberal feminism is a nuanced theorical strand, which takes different forms also in accordance with different audiences.

In sum, at the core of their battle, these early feminists put the creation of a common political platform. As the passages quoted above highlight, women claim their rights should be recognized by the powers to which they were subjected and which – by failing to properly consider them – subjected them. Interestingly, even while the solution envisaged lies in the achievement of a public, visible social stance, the authors of the *Declaration* are well aware of the complex nature of the power they question. What might be referred to as "patriarchy" is neither only a private domination nor exclusively a political supremacy: it is a capillary set of *mores* that are both private *and* political. Women should overcome fathers', brothers', husbands' grips *and* try to join the public arena that their fathers, brothers, husbands deemed to fall outside the domestic, feminine, realm.

The attempt at reaching a public status as the means for enhancing women's condition tells us something about the type of battle they were fighting. The insistence on the priority of being publicly and politically recognized might suggest the inconceivability of operating a change starting within the domestic bonds. Women should come out of the dark realm of the private sphere in order to obtain tools to enforce changes in the entire social structure, as well as in the political field that their private life was. If this awareness reached its peak with the feminist movements of the 1960s (as the rallying cry "the personal is political" demonstrates), the *verso* of the public scene appeared to be only a secondary issue in liberal programs.

An analysis of the reasons of the partial success of liberal feminist movements can be of help in unveiling the shortcomings of opportunity-oriented policies. Despite feminism's great formal achievements (from the elective franchise to the right to abortion), women's subjugation is far from being over. The condition of most women continues to be complicated: they are discriminated at work; suffer sexual harassment; are exposed to domestic violence, slavery, prostitution; are required to fit certain beauty and living standards.[8]

This all means that political enfranchisement cannot be regarded as the key to women's liberation. Instead, the most insidious problem lies at the heart of social structures, where changes "cannot occur [...] by edict" (Young 1990:152). The existing discrepancy between the formal liberation promoted in the legal text and its social impact fails to illuminate a condition of consolidate social inequality. This reasoning can be applied to a reading of opportunity-oriented policies. Norms inspired by this strategy are likely to reproduce a scheme that reinforces an unfair situation, by addressing it only partially. In this case, the law disregards the constitutive relationship between private and public and proves incapable of tackling deep-seated disparities.

Before continuing, I would like to emphasize that I am not supporting the naïve claim that laws aimed at opposing marginalization through the creation of political opportunities are inadequate or even harmful. Rather, I want to highlight the side effects of overlooking what is beyond the superficial manifestation

8 See the Commission on the Status of Women at http://www.unwomen.org/en/csw/previous-sessions/csw61-2017 (last accessed on 19 September 2018).

of political exclusion. Opportunity-oriented strategies run the risk of denying the contextual differences that feed multifarious forms of oppression. Thereby, "[e]quality law in its mainstream form cannot address the most systematic social disadvantages" (MacKinnon 2006:73). The extension of a model designed in accordance with specific standards obscures many of the variables that might trigger marginalization and address only specific manifestations of inequality. In other words, such measures fail to unroot the social factors that in non-mainstream real-life situations nurture unfairness. Because of this scarce sensitivity to the private sphere and the consequent tendency to endorse and refer to a mainstream model, opportunity-oriented policies are content with opening (at least on paper) dominant positions to marginalized individuals. The right to vote can exemplify this mechanism: while endowing every citizen with the formal possibility of participation, enfranchisement does not take into account difficulties that hamper an actual participation. It does not support a fair access to education, media, nor does it ascertain the real-life opportunities of poor women or women in a disadvantaged condition. It does not face disparity, it only pursues equality. But as Vittorio Bufacchi (2012) observes, equality has only one face, injustice has too many. Short of far-reaching operations that scrutinize the heart of the social context, the opening of public positions does not actively help certain categories to be included in political processes.

Based on what I have argued so far, the first model fails to address the specific needs of certain groups of people and implements indirectly discriminatory norms, creating systemic marginalization. Feminist scholars have largely debated on the outcomes of a double-edged legal intervention which ends up involuntarily supporting processes of social exclusions. Among others, the work of Catharine MacKinnon (1987, 1989) casts light on the discriminatory dimensions that might be reinforced through the annexation of conservative and traditional social structure in the legal body. These dimensions can be summed up as the distinction between public and private, the naturalization of dominance as difference, a mistaken account of coercion, and the creation and spread of cultural prejudices (MacKinnon 1989). Although MacKinnon seems to put these four dimensions on the same level, I would like to insist on the priority of the first one over the others, for the others find their strength in the separation of the private and the public spheres, that is, in the creation of two separated systems of values, internally regulated and placed in a hierarchical connection. It will then be useful to clarify some features of the distinction between the private and the public, according to MacKinnon who devotes a great part of her reflection to this topic and, on the basis of it, deploys a radical theory of the state.

In her distinctive style, MacKinnon presents a systematic reading of inequality and democratic institutions. At the core of her argument lies the idea that certain subjectivities cannot be addressed by state law because of their *difference*, or better, because of a *distinction* (MacKinnon 1987:32): a distinction that pertains to a cluster of sedimented gendered norms, that is, something that belongs to socio-historical dynamics and divisions of roles, prejudices contingent on the social articulation of sexuality.[9] Distinction creates a misperception since it contrasts with the idea of equality promulgated in and by the law. Such contrast is never solved, rather distinction does not find place in those norms that aim at promoting equality. This misperception (originated in social prejudices) penetrates the law insofar as it is modelled on specific structures where strong hierarchies endure. In MacKinnon's account, the legislative tool exerts a constructive power on the cultural and symbolic spheres, and consequently, it influences and structures them. It is possible, then, to envisage the vicious circles generated in this mechanism. The state emerges out of a highly connoted context and its structure reflects this in its redoubling: the perpetration of the initial order is nourished by the law and the state legal system benefits from the social stability it relies on and perpetrates (MacKinnon 2006:4). In this vicious circle, marginalized groups are *translated into* the law (and not *addressed by* the law) and remain unreal to power, falling outside the purview of short-sighted institutions.

This mechanism can hardly be challenged from a non-political space, as the domestic, private realm to which women historically belong. The main danger of a liberal strategy to approach equality (to treat "likes alike and unlikes unlike") is to carve out a space of non-interference, the establishment of a gap between the private and the public.[10] In this context, the public is subjected to the control of the state, whereas all that dwells in the private realm, and is considered to be licit, is allowed and above all, kept outside the reach of the law. At the same time, what is licit (and legitimated) comes to be delineated in light of the experience and perception of a dominant class, with the consequence that what is licit is deeply related to hegemonic identities. In a situation in which state institutions support and foster distinctive features which pertain to a dominant model there is not much leeway for non-hegemonic subjectivities to get a foothold in the political system, even if they appear to be legally encouraged to do so.

The elision of the private dimension concerns not only discrimination related to gender and sex, but broadly affects marginalized realities. The effectiveness of inclusive political strategies is reduced by this effacement that happens, as I noticed above, to reinforce and perpetrate an exclusionary setting. The rootedness of a system of signifiers, where standards and traditions are elevated to the status of naturalized norms depicting normality, however, impacts also on the possibility of rearticulating the relation between the private and the public sphere. In other words, even when – in a regimen shaped on the model of opportunities/public participation – the legislator addresses a case that typically pertains to the private domain, she will apply standards and measures that misread or misinterpret this event. This is due to the fact that in such a model, experiences (both private and public) tend to be read in terms of formal equality. In a

9 MacKinnon seems not to be interested in the distinction between gender as a cultural product and sexuality as a physical characteristic, see Brown (1989).

10 In providing a reconstruction of MacKinnon's claims, I will follow her examples and case studies (which are mostly centred on women); nonetheless, I regard the case of women as paradigmatic of all kinds of marginalization. I will therefore indicate when a narrower interpretation is needed.

scheme that praises the abstractness of a citizen, there is no place for considering how individual subjects can be affected personally by some events and thus, it is impossible to imagine a legal form of recognition that goes beyond an equality articulated as sameness.

The pre-eminence of the public rationality, within which any subject is – in the eye of the law – the manifestation of an abstract element of the polity (the citizen), conceals the legal relevance of private relationships and affections, personal choices and possibilities. In this sense, an approach linked to and contingent upon, a liberal, abstract idea of equality eventuates both in a poor comprehension of what MacKinnon defines "distinction" and in the incapacity of modifying existent social hierarchies, that constitute the ground of inequality.

A much-debated example of the way in which the implementation of this system lacks the possibility of understanding the importance of private experiences to overcome oppression concerns legal measures on rape. MacKinnon (1993, 2006) herself devotes many studies to rape law. In many legislations,[11] for a forced sexual intercourse to be considered (and pursued) as sexual assault, penetration must have occurred. The assessment of sexual assault is carried out by using a one-sided scale: sexual intercourses are evaluated from an utterly male perspective, leaving no room for a more nuanced comprehension of it.[12] In much the same vein, many jurisdictions apply biased parameters for assessing sex-related offenses; for instance, until 1981, the Italian law considered sexual violence and rape as crimes *against the public moral and public decency*, which denied any value to the person (usually a female person) subjected to harassment.

In this scenario, it appears clear that the greatest difficulty in treating problems concerning marginalization is the structure of the law itself (see MacKinnon 1989:171–237). In the face of it, even if the legislator modifies single laws by taking into account private experiences, such modifications have effects on

11 See the reports of Equality Now https://www.equalitynow.org/the_global_rape_epidemic_campaign?locale=en (last accessed on 19 September 2018). For reports on rape and sexual assault in the world visit https://www.wessexscene.co.uk/international/2018/02/28/sca-magazine-how-do-laws-of-sexual-assault-differ-around-the-world-edited/ and https://www.washingtonpost.com/news/monkey-cage/wp/2015/02/11/how-laws-around-the-world-do-and-do-not-protect-women-from-violence/?noredirect=on&utm_term=.1d13adc894d1 (last accessed on 19 September 2018).

See, for e.g. the account of rape law around U.S. offered in the Pandora's Project website http://www.pandys.org/index.html (last accessed on 6 September 2018).

12 Even if not explicitly, Italian perception seems to share the centrality of masculine experience. In the report of a notorious rape trial we can read: "PRESIDENT: You personally stopped at the first stage [...] that is, you didn't have a real intercourse; NOVELLI: No, I didn't have any intercourse, or well [...], I put it into her mouth, and that's it. I didn't have an intercourse [...]; PROSECUTOR: I'd like to know if he ejaculated, that is, a complete coitus or not. [...]; *NOVELLI:* [...] ***I didn't have a complete coitus;*** PRESIDENT: But did you manage to reach the pleasure?; *NOVELLI: Yes, in that moment [...]*; president: Enough, enough; It's enough" (Belmonti et al. 1980:26–27). The questioning, focused on the re-enactment of the rape, lingered on the definition of "a complete intercourse", which is characterized as based on vaginal penetration and ejaculation. The woman's experience is completely obliterated in this description.

insulated fact-types and leave its fundamental biases untouched. Specific legal amendments, aimed at reconfiguring distinct aspects of the public-political sphere, fail to challenge the roots of marginalization, avoiding any structural modification of an unfair system.[13]

MacKinnon's reflections can be considered as a case in point, useful to reveal some of the dynamics that underlie the opportunity-oriented model: her insights reveal the basic outcomes of the binary division between public and private. On the one hand, she highlights that the law

> often collaborates by making an unusual or extreme form of a common violation illegal, so that what is illegal almost never happens, yet the law appears to stand against the violation. Victims are thereby ideologically rendered appropriate to their treatment, the unequal treatment serving to confirm their ontological status as lesser human. *When nothing is done, the treatment, and social status accordingly, confirm and create who one is.* (MacKinnon 2006:3–4, emphasis added)

In a situation of general unfairness, when the law targets marginalized people, law itself can contribute to confining them in a condition of deficiency, or, as the author says, to make them "lesser humans".[14] On the other hand, she submits that one of the most deceptive consequences of this division is what can be referred to as "euphemization" (Bourdieu 1991),[15] a mechanism at work in the shift that occurs in the narration of public and private crimes. In Pierre Bourdieu's account, "the euphemistic discourse is less duplicity and hypocrisy than denial" and becomes "a discourse which is able to assure the coexistence of opposites" in a context where "domination and discrimination cannot be exercised directly" (Blackledge 2005:218). In much the same way, hegemonic narratives about

13 Such deep-rooted unfairness is typical of liberal and neo-liberal political systems, in which the private/public division is well established. An example of the liberal reasoning and its inappropriateness is detectable in the debate between Avv. Tina Lagostena Bassi and the Court in the trial mentioned above. The defender, Avv. Lagostena Bassi, asked just one *lira* in compensation for the harm caused to her assisted who had been the victim of a group-rape. With this provocative gesture, Langostena Bassi wanted to denounce a system that – by the means of *pecuniary reparation* – debases rape and its consequences on women's life. In her speech, the defender clearly states that rape is not measurable:

> [W]e will ask for a symbolic *lira* as compensation, as the harm suffered by a raped girl is incommensurable, and cannot be compensated with a bribe, […] because we, women, believe this well-established practice is extremely offensive […] is incommensurable the harm a woman suffers when she is raped. (Belmonti et al. 1980:9–11)

14 Note that MacKinnnon herself indicates the ambiguous status of equality laws, inasmuch as being protected by the law says something about one's position in the social realm: one's need for a law that rescues oneself from marginalization means that *if it were not for the law*, her position would be an abject one. See also Brown (2000).

15 The employment of this Bourdieusian term is part of a personal reconstruction of MacKinnon's thought, since she does not explicitly refer to the French author in dealing with these questions. On the contrary, Bourdieu (1998) approvingly cites MacKinnon in *La domination masculine*.

crimes committed in the private sphere are articulated by using terms, words and locutions which understate these offenses. This process results in the constitution of two systems of values (a "double standard", as MacKinnon calls it) for estimating and judging the two spheres. A stunning proof of this disparity is the difference in judicial treatment of violation and torture (see MacKinnon 2006).[16] Euphemization here, takes the form of an unalike consideration of facts performed by using a different cluster of terms for expressing similar things that occurred in different settings.

Euphemization along with victimization produces an attitude that naturalizes dominance as difference. In fact, both tendencies give rise to a vertical relation in which a group objectifies the other by granting itself a preeminent position and, at the same time, by manipulating processes of knowledge production and the distribution of power. By defining one group as conforming to the norm and perceiving all the subjects who do not belong to that group as defective, the essence of discrimination comes to be instilled in the social realm. When a standard is posed, "to be an equal, you must be the same as whoever sets the dominant standards" (MacKinnon 2006:26). In this context, prejudices are not unlikely to retain a huge value and to foster resilient unfair behaviours against discriminated populations. MacKinnon's line of reasoning provides further evidence that the basic mechanism of opportunity-oriented policies is inadequate to tackle widespread biases against marginalized people: one's being admitted to the public sphere does not amount to one's being accepted in it or to one's being able to take advantage of its mechanisms and practices.

The author pinpoints a further dimension along which domination is exerted on marginalized strands of the citizenry, which she defines as the mystification of consent, that is, an arbitrary misperception of coercion and its slippage into consent. In many of her works, she shows how, in the case of women, this dimension finds its paradigmatic form not only in rape but also in mainstream pornographic representations.[17] For her, these cases follow the same pattern (and influence their respective outcomes)[18] by depicting the lowest pole of the

16 If we want to refer again to concrete examples, we can take the notorious Italian case usually called "*Massacro del Circeo*" (massacre of the Circeo – a seaside resort in the south of Latium), in which two girls were segregated for several days, battered and violated (one of the two drown in a bath tub) and the murderers have been set free before the end of the punishment.

17 I am here referring to mainstream porn. In the last decade, a new trend has emerged: postporn, that is, the reappropriation of porn on the part of queer film-makers. The aim of these works and performances is to represent a sexuality freed from the heterosexual, sexist and objectifying cluster of symbols and practices that hallmark mainstream porn. Postporn is, then, first and foremost a political tool, see Borghi (2012).

18 Mackinnon (1993:30–31) remarks:

> Discrimination does not divide into acts on one side and speech on the other. [...] Acts speak. In the context of social inequality, so-called speech can be an exercise of power which constructs the social reality in which people live, from objectification to genocide. The words and images are either direct incidents of such acts, such as making pornography or requiring Jews to wear yellow stars, or are connected to them, whether immediately,

hierarchy as moulded on the desires of the prevailing one. The subjected party is considered to be the embodied desire of the dominant subject and, for this reason, it does not have the possibility of laying their own claims or maintaining their own choices. In MacKinnon's (1993:6 and 29 ff) perspective, "you learn that speech is not what you say but what your abusers do to you", which means that if you find yourself "at the bottom" of social hierarchies, you are exposed to a constant re-modulation of your claims. The pattern of mainstream pornography (in which the position of the woman is always a position of oppression *and* consent)[19] is replicated in real life and manifested through the total annihilation of women's claims. This process can also be viewed through the lenses of euphemization, in that it is based on a systematic shift between meanings. In this sense, some conducts might escape legal sanctions by being concealed under ambiguous characterization. This occurs, for instance, when sexual harassment is reported as "flirting" (Fricker 2006) or domestic violence as normal intercourse between a man and his wife.

This condition has been defined by Rae Langton as an "illocutionary disablement". Langton (1993:315) portrays illocutionary disablement as the hardest form of silencing, in that it impacts on the validity claims of one's speech act. Acts of dissent performed by marginalized individuals are made unspeakable not simply by depriving speech of its intended illocutionary force, but by replacing it with antithetic claims. In cases such as pornography, or forced sexual intercourse, women's speech is soaked up by a mechanism of systematic misunderstanding. The rules of the game – namely, those pointed out by MacKinnon – ascribe to women a crystallized role, which they have to accept in order to play a part in the broader social game. In this context, "consent is the only thing a woman can do with her words in this game" (Langton 1993:324). This form of oppression ensnares women in a condition of unspeakability, which thrusts their voice in the light of the dominator's desires and makes them understandable only in that light. Policy measures that fail to come to terms with this less visible dimension of marginalization fail to give an account of the actual competences that one must acquire in order for her to participate in the public life.

This scenario can be portrayed as a condition of "epistemic disadvantage" (Fricker 2006) that affects marginalized individuals' communicative skills both at a most visible level of public interaction and at a more personal,[20] intimate one. This is evidence that, contrary to a widespread but shallow perception of

linearly, and directly, or in more complicated extended ways. [...] Words are images of how people are placed in hierarchies, how social stratification is made to seem inevitable and right, how feelings of inferiority and superiority are engendered, and how indifference to violence against those on the bottom is rationalized and normalized.

19 I use the term "consent" because women in pornography are depicted in an attitude of eternal agreement, but – given the fact that even their "no" means "yes" (MacKinnon 2006) – this agreement should be seen as a coercion. Nonetheless, the rules of the game are such that coercion is relished by the dominated, in that no matter what they say to be wanting, they seek to be dominated by men and appreciate it.

20 For a broader reflection on this topic, see Young (2000).

marginalization as mere exclusion, marginalization is a two-layered condition. Exclusion is just one of the possible aspects of a wider phenomenon which includes subtler modulations such as what I may call "oppression-in-acceptance",[21] whereby groups or subjects are aggrieved by systematic disrepute. The right to political participation that opportunity-oriented policies provide them with, risks to be turned into the meaningless exercise of extended administrative rights. Indeed, marginalized people (whether allowed to engage in political activities or not)[22] have a minimal impact on the institutional agenda. Young regards shortcomings of this sort of institutional politics as cases in which minorities become "politically negligible". Among these cases, the author enumerates the impossibility of getting acquainted with the set of actual, unwritten rules that governs the "political game". The importance of handling a "proper rhetoric" or of showing "appropriate behaviours" (e.g. respectively how to bring out issues or which procedures to follow) are key means to be taken into account in people's behaviour within the public forum. Reading this structure through a Bourdieusian grid allows taking a further step: if the social system is structured as a "market", and "capitals" are the means necessary to gain access to it, then the inaptitude that stems from one's cognitive disablement gets perpetuated by one's position in the social system.

In sum, it is possible to describe the multilayered social condition of marginalized subjects as one that has its kernel in three kinds of deficiency: a lack of horizon, which is conceivable as a hermeneutic shortage that marginalizes and segregates; a lack of terms, which can be considered as the inaccessibility of the public space, that is, the symbolically violent neglect of certain experiences; and a lack of power, or better, the systemic oppression that derives from powerlessness. In an ascending order, the former has to do with the development of individual capacities, while the latter has to do with the configuration of the social realm as a whole.

21 Here I rely on the terms used by Young (2000) in her account of the multiple sides of marginalization.

22 Needless to say, in a highly democratic context, marginalized people will not be prevented, for example, from exercising their right to vote. The analysis I am providing here suggests the development of a wider concatenation of events (which can be explained with recourse to Fricker's [2006] interpretation of cognitive disablement) that traps marginalized people in a vicious circle. On the one hand, they are deprived of a set of basic competences necessary for them to employ political tools; on the other hand, scarce participation precludes them from obtaining visibility.

2 Model 2

Capability-based policies

An alternative approach to marginalization, somewhat opposite to the one discussed above, is taken up by those policies that seek to promote inclusion by working on specific aspects of an individuals' private life. Such strategies, which I refer to as "capability-based" build on the idea that marginalization can be defeated only by considering differences. While opportunity-oriented policies seek to achieve inclusion through the creation of a "levelling" political platform, mostly blind to all private differentials of power (class, race, gender, education), capability-based policies emphasize the need to do justice to the heterogeneity of human variance to develop a system in which equality does not aim at sameness, but emerges from the recognition of an innate, inescapable and irreducible diversity.

Political equality is portrayed as something that the subject *gains access to* in her individual experience. It takes the form of a fair distribution of social possibilities and gives way to an idea of empowerment as *enactment*. While political participation was the possibility of accessing pregiven tasks, these policies aim at creating an environment in which everyone can realize herself by following their own inclinations and interests. Rather than promoting a univocal way of being engaged in (or addressed by) the political sphere and the democratic processes, capabilities-based programmes intend to valorize differences and accommodate them in a nuanced understanding of what political participation entails. This group of policies expands the scope of the law to produce juridico-political instruments aimed at promoting social interaction and fostering personal development. Therefore, public institutions are called upon to invest resources on the improvement of individuals' personal conditions, rather than simply granting formal access to political procedures. This latter solution in fact has been demonstrated as necessary but ineffective, since it ignores the social dimension of marginalization and obliterates the differences among (marginalized) people. In the capability-based approach, political institutions are mainly required to enact a special form of "redistributive" politics, one that focuses on the quality of life. Redistributing, then, does not concern the mere allocation of material resources but consists in identifying and undermining enduring inequalities that lie in the social domain and are reproduced therein.

To carry out this task, policymakers should take into consideration human differences and social differentials, the heterogeneity of interests, choices and desires, the private resources to realize personal goals, the importance of investing these resources and one's own efforts not only to achieve individual utility, but to reach a well-being that unfolds into social interactions and the constitution of a fair, inclusive context (see Sen 1992:1–11).

The first task of this type of inclusive policies is to challenge pervasive inequality by tackling social circumstances that curb and poison the individual capacity to reach what can be seen as a basic quality. The evaluation of marginalization cannot proceed by the appraisal of formal opportunities. Rather, it should consider several features that affect individual lives. Starting with an assessment of "*focal variables*" (Sen 1992:20), from the more general (the environment, both social and natural), to the more specific (personal characteristics, income and wealth, education, liberties, rights), capability-based inclusive policies should foster the *development* and *exercise* of different, personal and context-dependent *capabilities.*

The political expression of this paradigm results in a delineation of inclusion as the consolidation of a variegated and nuanced political community, where everyone can find their place and live their life at its best. Equality, in this case, emerges as inherently linked to justice:

> Democracy has to be judged not just by the institutions that formally exist but by the extent to which different voices from diverse sections of the people can actually be heard [...] [and thus it] is not seen simply in terms of the setting up of some specific institutions (like a democratic global government or global elections), but in terms of the possibility and reach of public reasoning. (Sen 2010:xiii)

In this perspective, the concept of justice overlaps with the concept of equality (that, in turn, loses any connection with the notions of sameness and identity) and expresses a very broad political commitment. Democracy, in order to be *just*, has to take into *equal* consideration the broadest amounts of subjects. To this end, more than relying on the idea of treating people *in the same way and with the same means*, in a capability-based approach the instance of "equality" is reshaped in terms of *efficiency*: to defeat marginalization, people must be treated in accordance with their personal conditions.

This can be done only by promoting a political model that "takes *each person as an end*" (Nussbaum 2011:18). In this sense, capability-based strategy informs a kind of politics

> *focused on choice or freedom*, holding that the crucial good societies should be promoting for their people is a set of opportunities, or substantial freedoms [...]. [A politics that] [...] commits itself to respect for people's powers of self-definition. [This] approach is resolutely *pluralist about value* [...]. Finally, [it] is *concerned with entrenched social injustice and inequality* [...].

> It ascribes an urgent *task to government and public policy* – namely, to improve the quality of life for all people as defined by their capabilities. (Nussbaum 2011:18–19)

Before continuing to illustrate the key concept of "capability" and see how it fits in the model I am presenting here, I want to draw attention to a crucial shift that results from focusing on personal lives and private achievements. The emphasis on single *human experiences* complexifies the approach to inclusion. So much so that, in a capability-based model, strategies to achieve inclusion appear far more demanding than in other strategies that rest upon simplification. As we have seen, procedures informed by opportunity-oriented policies are strictly linked to the abstraction of a subject of law (the citizen) and the consequent determination of areas of interests that should affect her life. Taking as a model, an abstract figure implies the selection of a series of tools and instruments that would suit general circumstances. If this approach has the advantage of offering policymakers exact and straightforward criteria to operate in society, it certainly reduces the scope of inclusive policies to the promotion of general, non-assessable solutions. On the other hand, capability-based policies manifest the ambitious goal of providing a cluster of modulable answers to very specific and unforeseeable problems. In this perspective, laws structured along the line of capability-based policies address as their subject the "human being", a controversial concept suspended between nature and culture. Needless to say, the demarcation of such a dense subject of law requires a keener theoretical effort. While "the citizen" is delineated through recourse to a political constitution (that indicates *who* has to be considered politically significant), the definition of a human being involves a great theoretical effort to retrieve and indicate its essential characteristics.

The bold philosophical premises on which this approach relies can be related to philosophical and economic theories that from 1980s came to the fore as an alternative way of conceiving welfare economics and politics: the Capability Approach. Firstly deployed by Amartya Sen as an economic theory and then philosophically developed by Martha Nussbaum, the Capability Approach has gained importance in many domains, exerting great impact on the contemporary political debate.

In its earlier formulations, Sen expounds the idea that political order is ultimately dependent on the "kind of creature we are" (Sen 2010:169–170). Human beings and their features are taken as the foundational stone of a political society and for that reason, social structures and political systems have to be "dependent on our sense organs, and our brains, and other human bodily capacities" (Sen 2010:169). Political systems should provide workable solutions to concrete problems and consequently constitute a fairer societal structure. The subject to which capability-oriented policies are targeted takes the form of an individual merged in a net of cultural influences and relationships, which marks her connection and position her in a social environment. Human beings are influenced not only by the context they inhabit, but also by a thorough difference depending on age, gender, education, class, features and genetic endowments, attitudes, desires, expectations and tendencies. In other words, human beings "are diverse, but diverse in different ways" (Sen 1992:85).

How can a political model account for these endless, fluctuating, unexpected variations? What does it mean to choose the "human being" in its extreme variability as the subject of law? Things might get very complicated for policymakers, if it were not for an element, as thin as heavy. Human beings are all diverse, *but they are all human.* In this sense, supporters of the Capability Approach presuppose a substratum, an essential core on which variables are engraved. Social connections, relationships, desires, possibilities and goals in their similarities reveal a shared *human nature.* On one side, this nature sets expectations concerning people's spectrum of ethical, cognitive and emotive attitudes. Human beings are characterized by a common rational orientation and an original disposition to sympathy (see e.g. Sen 2010:143). Moreover, they share a minimal "human core" that orientates the delineation of a basic set of "substantial freedoms" (see Nussbaum 2011; Sen 1999). On the other, it allows to identify the lines along which inclusive policies might unfold. On the basis of the recognition of general patterns and structures that belong to all human beings, it is possible to draw a list of capabilities and functionings, that is, a list of what a person can aspire, and which are the achievements that contribute, to human well-being and, thus, have to be supported by institutions.

In Sen's account, functions and capabilities consist "in beings and doings" (Sen 1992:39) and the capability to make them function. While functionings are *achievements* that increase the well-being of a person, capabilities are "vectors of functionings" and reflect the "persons' freedom to choose from possible livings" (40). Both are constituent elements of a person's well-being and yet they not only serve the purpose of evaluating a living condition; in fact, in being considered as constitutive and essential functions of a human life, they also answer the question of what a *good life* looks like. In Sen's words, for example, the "relevant functionings" comprise not only of "elementary things as being adequately nourished, being in good health, avoiding escapable morbidity and premature mortality, etc.", but also include "more complex achievements such as being happy, having self-respect, taking part in the life of the community, and so on". Happiness, self-respect as well as participating in a community are indicated as ciphers of a good, fulfilling life. However, in listing some of the traits that might characterize a good life, Sen is indicating a general process of isolation of essential features that *has to* structure a human life. In much the same way, Nussbaum (2003b, 2006) considers capabilities and functionings as the source of an inclusive social context. They postulate the felicitous development of a human life. Personal development is the path towards fairness and equality, that is, towards inclusion, the ultimate outcome of social justice.

Institutions are called upon for supporting the achievement of individual constructive and empowering choices and goals that are firmly linked to the list of human capabilities and functionings. Needless to say, capabilities and functionings have to be individuated and listed in order to provide a guide for policymakers. The list of capabilities (and consequently, the range of possible functionings, endorsed and supported by the state) has to be found, in Nussbaum's opinion, through a *rational process*, that is, a logical procedure that inherently guarantees the validity of the list itself, because it can be retraced by every *rational being* and mirrors a common understanding of the human good. In this framework, cultural diversity and personal variance are still considered as the felicitous flourishing of *human lives*. This makes the subject of capability-based policies general and unique, definite and undefinable, naturalized and exposed to cultural fluctuations at the same time.

Along with the premise of humanity as a unifying guideline to set up inclusive strategies, a political approach that resonates with the Capability Theory praises variance. While individual differences remain on the background in the delineation of a list of functionings that has to be fostered, environmental and social differences constitute another main element to consider. Governments should, in fact, secure capabilities in accordance with the specific (natural, economic and political) history of every country as well as with the social conditions of the communities that compose its fabric.

To sum up, the capability-based approach advocates the protection of a narrow cluster of liberties and rights but leaves a wide leeway in terms of which kind of norms should support them. Political institutions are required to comply with a set of pre-political principles that can be shaped in accordance with the specific variables of single national contexts. Redistributive patterns, the safeguards of minorities, equal treatment in terms of opportunities and private liberties are influenced by the general conditions of the country. On the basis of a constant assessment of the actual conditions in which capability-based strategies have to be implemented, it is possible to set an ambitious but not utopic threshold of well-being (see Villani 2012), which should take into account what is deemed to be the basic cluster of human rights, with regard to the centrality of the broadest inclusion. In this sense, this threshold is always "multiple", since it has to combine several indexes to provide the fairer allocation of resources in accordance with diverse potentialities (Wolf and de-Shalit 2007:91–94). Institutions are thus engaged in implementing a consistent set of rights that, on one side, should protect liberties derived from the ratified list of capabilities and, on the other, should assist those who are not able to reach one or more functionings by supplying support.

In addition, institutions are called upon to secure a smooth transition between capabilities and functionings, following the assumption that a lack of functionings is not necessarily linked to a lack of innate abilities, as the former might be the outcome of an unfair distribution of social, material or cognitive opportunities. If we look back at the case of opportunity-oriented policies, it is possible to grasp how a distinctive discrepancy of personal possibilities can easily slip into an external impediment: the extension of the right to vote (intended as the outcome of a fair distribution of political rights) does not always result in the actual engagement of a citizen. As I observed above, guaranteeing a right is a necessary but not sufficient condition for achieving political participation. To be effective, the provision of an opportunity must proceed from the nourishment of personal capabilities. The improvement of individuals' conditions constitutes the essential difference between the capabilities approach and other political theories that, despite the common objective of dismantling marginalization, overlook individuals' and socio-contextual features that trigger the mechanism of social exclusion.

In opposition to accounts that tend to overlook the social context to provide an all-purpose standard solution, policies inspired by the capability approach tend to be organized on the basis of a sound knowledge of the sociocultural context of a given country. Central to the definition of policy lines of intervention is an enquiry that gathers the analysis of sociopolitical structures and individuals' private experiences. By promoting a pluralistic approach to marginalization, capabilities-based policies promote inclusion by addressing the complex interlacement of multiple strategies.

A convincing "capabilist" portrayal of the interconnection among disadvantages is offered by Jonathan Wolff and Anver de-Shalit (2007). The authors carry out a closer analysis of specific disadvantages that might generate contexts of marginalization or that might originate from them. In order to do so, they draw on, and amend,[1] Nussbaum's list of capabilities so as to provide an overview of conditions that usually lead some minor strands of the population to live below an acceptable threshold of well-being. In their work, Wolf and de-Shalit undertake a twofold task: on the one hand, they outline a detailed description of specific situations, while, on the other hand, they implicitly provide a general method for investigating and evaluating the fragmented reality of disadvantage. The observation of marginalized situations and their shared traits leads the authors to determine which elements policymakers should monitor in order to find a remedy to marginalization. First, Wolf and de-Shalit claim that interventions should be effective in breaking the chain of difficulties that usually affect marginalized people. Such an effort is particularly important because intertwined disadvantages might generate what they refer to as a situation of "corrosive disadvantages", in which the subject is not able to overcome the oppressive scenario she is stuck in, since she is trapped in a recursive state of urgency. This state implies that those who are involved in dynamics of corrosive disadvantage miss the opportunity and resources both for coping with the whole situation and for tackling single problematic areas of their lives. The failure of any strategy of improvement is due to the lack of resources that affects marginalized people's

1 The authors add to Nussbaum's list more capabilities retrieved through interviews, which prove key to understand central problems experienced by people in a disadvantaged situation. These are evidence of their orientation towards a more pragmatic reflection on how to tackle disadvantages can be find also in the empirical way used for testing the list itself. This solution is surely not paternalistic (as some of the outcomes of Nussbaum's version might be), but has as its main flaw the impossibility to overstep the restricted self-narrations provided by those who are involved in miserable situations. A hint of the importance of Wolf and de-Shalit's added functionings can be found in the work of Mariana Valverde (2012) who discusses cases of trials in which foreign people unable to speak the language of the country were involved.

lives, such that they cannot progress with their own means. This intricate system can exert an influence at multiple levels, since what is lacking is not just one kind of resources. Financial shortage can be intermingled with educational deficiencies or with the unavailability of services in a single area, as well as with the absence of a net of relationships or the failed familiarization with the surrounding environment. In this sense, material scarcity can be the superficial index of deeper deprivations, like in the cases described by Sendhil Mullainathan and Eldar Shafir (2013), in which invalidating pecuniary conditions mirror similar situations of time scarcity and the other way around. On this account, the psychological response to one type of scarcity influences the overall behaviour of a subject, to the extent that it provokes a muddled reaction to everyday situations, one that worsens original conditions of disadvantage and heightens difficulties.

The eradication of clusters of corrosive disadvantages has its counterpart in the promotion of "fertile functionings". Against the weakening process engendered by overlapping variables, fertile functionings ignite a virtuous circle in which basic functionings are secured and improved. The development of such a favourable condition is tied to the creation of productive services and institutions directed at fostering everyone's well-being and at being accessible by everyone.

In short, Wolf and de-Shalit promote a strategy of inclusion based on three pillars: an empirical examination of *individuals' genuine capabilities* and of *functionings derived from them*; an account of *social complexities*[2] and an accurate identification of the conditions that could cause a backlash (exposing people who overcame their condition of disadvantage to a further decline), with a view on *minimizing risks of losing functionings.* The latter is at the basis of any effective capability-based policy, in that "a person's prospect of achieving and sustaining a level of functioning should they attempt to do so" (Wolf and de-Shalit 2007:72) is necessary to propel change. In opposition to "resourcist" or "welfarist" and other political strategies based on the reallocation of resources for contrasting marginalization, the last point indicated by Wolf and de-Shalit constitutes the signature feature of capability-based policies. Such model raises awareness on the inefficacy of scattered, momentary resolutions. It highlights that a lack of possibility constitutes an insurmountable obstacle, because it elicits the subjects' feeling of being incapable of accomplishing any "expected" results.

In a capability-based model, thus, policymakers are doomed to uphold a pluralistic approach to foresee most of the possible intersections and interrelations among policies, individual commitment and social resilience.

To sum up, the main features of a capability-based approach are: the crucial role played by the identification of context-specific capabilities and functionings

2 A more comprehensive perspective can help in preventing interventions directed to some kinds of people to have a bad impact on different areas, so as to avoid that a practice for relieving a situation becomes detrimental to others who are in a disadvantaged position as well. A vey illustrative example can be found in a comparison between policies directed to people on the wheelchair (bigger sidewalks and thresholds, no obstacles on the streets, etc.) and the ones directed to blind people (tactile indicators both vertical and horizontal).

to set up political goals and inclusive strategies; the centrality of the notion of subjects of law as human beings, that is, as beings composed by (cultural and natural) variables, but always sharing a common essential and recognizable core; an understanding of democratic processes and institutions as mainly bound to serve an associative role, with a strong focus on individuals and their needs, rather than simply as processes that fulfil governmental tasks; a specific consideration of justice, that takes the form of an equality-in-difference.

The system that follows from these general lines appears as inherently double. Capability-based model is haunted by a tension between shared dispositions that belong to stable, coherent human beings and the embracement of different inclination (culturally/socially shaped) of human subjects. Democratic inclusion – as intended by capability-based policies – requests each subject to hold rights and privileges in relation to their functionings and capabilities. However, in order to fully consider human variables, any decision-making process has to postulate an essential specificity of human beings. Humanity is not modified by any cultural inclination, nor can it be altered by physical or material differences. Variables are, in this scenario, reduced to superficial variations.

Interestingly, both Nussbaum and Sen often recall an idea of the human being as participating of reason. According to Nussbaum, it is reason that allows us to draw a list of capabilities that overcomes any possible hurdle or scepticism. According to Sen, it is reason the foundational stone of a social and political inclination, of these feelings and tendencies that make us – as human beings – oriented towards surpassing the contingency of our social, political, personal position to embrace a vaster, kinder way of being a part of a political community that goes beyond the here and now:

> An adult competent person has the ability to question what has been taught to her [...]. While circumstances may not encourage a person to do such questioning, *the ability to doubt and to question is within each person's capacity*. Indeed, it is not absurd to claim that being able to doubt is one of the things *that make us human beings*, rather than unquestioning animals. (Sen 1997:24, emphasis added)

By centring a theory on the idea that *all* human beings are born alike (at least for what concerns their *potentials*) and thinking inequality as caused only by unfair social structures, Sen and the supporters of a capabilist model actually *exclude* from their perspective all those whose capabilities do not reflect standardized ones. The quoted passage, for instance, makes sense of the location of a rational human nature at the core of inclusive democratic processes, which implies the confinement of individual variables to a superficial level. In this way, inclusion itself ultimately relies on an implicit banishment of those realities which fall out of a standardized human figure.

This foundational element is not alien to the theoretical assumptions explicitly displayed in Sen's work. Even if more indirectly, the institutional approach to capabilities promoted by Nussbaum, and by the other authors analyzed so far, is completely premised on the positioning of a natural set of (specifically) human traits. On her account, Nussbaum links capabilities to a set of functionings and values that "however culturally inflected, exceed any cultural influence and are ascribable to human nature" (Botti 2013:111). The author stresses the importance of revealing such intrinsic feature as "too important to be left to whim and caprice, or even to the dictates of a cultural tradition" (Nussbaum 2003a:47). In this sense, the list of functionings presented by the author reduces differences to bare *accidents* which are posed, engraved and apposed on a central, static, shared human core. In fact, in her list, Nussbaum (2003a:57) introduces a set of binding traits, which are meant to guide the formulation of policies aimed at promoting and reinforcing everyone's capabilities. Accordingly, policies would work for the improvement of certain functionings and the enhancement of determinate features. These functionings are "culture-neutral", and thus are displayed by every human being, in spite of individuals' positioned choices, which are doomed to be influenced by cultural belongings and social background (see Botti 2013:112–113).

This is evidence that at the core of the capabilities-based paradigm lies a dangerous shift between the "descriptive/assertive plan" and the "normative plan" (Marzocchi 2004:90). The delineation of a clear-cut cluster of needs, which are considered to be valuable in the light of a pregiven human nature (Marzocchi 2004:88–92), is conducive to the creation of a political structure based on a standardized, stable subject. This idea cannot but be partial and exclusive, for, if potentialities and features constituting the kernel of humanity are drawn out of an observation of widespread conducts, then, the list will inevitably reify a generalized understanding of *how* to be human.

As a result, this univocal understanding of human nature supports the creation of policies aimed at improving only *certain* conditions. This is detrimental for all those subjects who are most likely to suffer from a form of marginalization. People who do not display the essential capabilities (and thus cannot aspire to achieve basic functionings)[3] would cope with difficulty with any program aimed at relieving marginalization, in that they would be considered not suitable for partaking actively in the political community as advocates of capability-based approaches intend it.

In sum, capability-oriented policies involve a high degree of ambiguity. While it is true that the strategies adopted guarantee a more comprehensive perspective on the private sphere of marginalized realities and point at installing anti-discriminatory practices into everyday realities by supplying people with tools (from education to a web of supportive relationships) useful to reach autonomy and to give them the possibility to overcome marginalization with one's own resources. It is also true that this widespread form of inclusion is fashioned in such a way that it can reach only those who share some core features of the "hegemonic

3 Different is the case of those who do not *actively manifest* or *use* such capabilities as many debates on euthanasia and disability have shown, on this, see e.g. Formosa and Mackenzie (2014).

humanity". When a line between rationality, or other "human" characteristics and a political stance is drawn, those who fall out of a standardized idea struggle to see their position recognized as politically relevant. Notwithstanding the theoretical attempt to produce a perspective in which the notion of a human species, whose common features are shared, is merged with the notion of a democratic political structure, in which marginalization is channelled towards the acceptance of differences and mutual recognition, the capability-based model proves engulfed in an anthropocentric, highly normative paradigm. A pression towards excluding some variables is ineradicable. It inheres any system whose rules define who is considered part of the system, no matter how minimal, light, open these rules are. On account of that, in view of a broader inclusion, capabilities-based policies perpetrate the banishment of those who do not fit in hegemonic spaces.

An instance of this mechanism can be observed in the way in which the issue of disability is taken up in contemporary democracies, both at an organizational level (that is non-juridical) and at a more institutionalized one (the level of policies). People with disability experience a form of twofold marginalization, in which segregation is reinforced by the enactment of a deceitful control and a tendency to deny autonomy. In being considered "***diversamente abili***"[4] (to use a very infelicitous trope), people who do not correspond to physical and mental standards are ensnared in a structure that, on one side, considers them to be less suited to engage in everyday activities and, on the other, urges them to conform to alleged normal rhythms. In this sense, physical or mental impairments often play a little role in the constitution of the destitute situation that marks a disabled life: the main obstacles for overcoming marginalization are frequently allocated in the social realm. Somehow, the idea that underpins practices and regulations addressing people with disability is that they are not (even socially or lawfully) suitable to be considered agents, but can occupy only the role of patients, costumers, members of a liminal reality. In the case of people with disability, a strange replacement occurs: a silent deprivation of rights and agency is combined with a stiff control, constituted by imposed standards which ought to be met, and by a prejudiced consideration of their limits. In more pragmatic terms, the control exerted over people with disability deprives them of political tools and thus hampers a recognition of them as political agents.

Capabilities-based policies epitomize this tendency and inadvertently foster it, by pursuing an ideal of integration and inclusion based on normalization of non-conforming people, that is, based on the encouragement to achieve standard qualities and capacities. Promoted values of equality induce to consider certain forms of life as constantly inadequate, so as to perceive some people as constantly in need, in a "status of minority". This is true not only for those who present mental impairments,[5] but also for the ones who suffer from physical

4 Otherwise able, as people with disability are labelled in a "politically correct" Italian.

5 People with intellectual impairments are hardly thought of as active participants of an inclusive democracy. Many political theories that praise autonomy and reason as two core features of the political actor struggle to find a way to include these people.

handicaps. In both cases, imposed settlements are implemented while concealed under the rhetoric of help and care. In both cases, autonomy, self-organization and the possibility of choice are mostly taken away.[6] The enforcement of care and the idea of an everlasting dependency, put away people with disability not only from social life, but also from the concrete possibility of developing skills. They are caught in a circle: in being forced to be dependent, they are not allowed to claim autonomy.

Even if the assumptions that underlie such a structure have been disproved by the rising of new alternative accounts and narratives around disability, very little has changed in the routine of people with disability. After a brief presentation of the shift that occurred between a medical approach to disability and a social or interactional one, I will show how laws inspired by a capabilist approach can risk worsening the situation of the lives of people with disability and above all, can aggravate certain forms of exclusion.

As I have explained so far, capability-based policies pursue inclusion by trying to achieve functional social equality. To carry out this ambitious program, the legislator should resort to set up a redistribution of resources (whether material or not) and try to level differentials of possibilities. This can be obtained through the promotion of interventions oriented at either improving functionings or fostering capabilities. In the former case, attention is drawn to single subjects and interventions concern domains as education or social mobility. Instead, when directed at fostering capabilities, interventions aim at producing a more friendly and fairer environment. Since capabilities flourish in a fertile context, capability-based policies hold a strong connection with the creation of favourable social conditions. The shift of paradigm that leads from opportunity-oriented policies to the ones I am exploring here concerns the transformation of the subject of law in an embodied subject. The legislator operates around a figure constituted by some basic traits, who presents, at the same time, indefinite personal variables. However, in being considered *as an* embodied subject, the environment that surrounds her becomes extremely important for propounding inclusion.

Thus, in a capability-based approach not only personal variables and heterogeneous clusters of disadvantages should be taken into account. The attention of the legislators should indeed focus on the background, not only that which regards the general situation of the nation state, but also more narrow segments and structures within which personal lives unfold.

The need to consider the environment as a key element of one's own personal development has been thoroughly explored by Disability Studies scholars and

6 Forced sterilization of people with disability is still a widespread practice all over the world. Anyway, in some cases, medical interventions are even more invasive and annihilating, as in the case of the so-called "Pillow Angel Treatment", which presupposes hormonal treatments, breast removal, sterilization for people affected by static encephalopathy of unknown aetiology in order to "freeze" the patient's bodies at the age of 7 (or before), so as to avoid all the complications due to a grown body. For further details, visit the website edited by the first parents who used this method: www.pillowangel.org (last accessed November 2018).

activists. In particular, Disability Studies should be credited with the merit of having tackled the political value of a common understanding of disability as a mere consequence of physical and/or mental impairments.

The account of disability as a bodily condition, regarding only the personal dimension of life, encourages a medical perception of it and results in the neglect of its sociopolitical side (see e.g. Medeghini 2013; Monceri 2012; Onnis 2013; Stiker 1997). This view, largely supported by the so-called "medical model" (see e.g. Mitchell 1999; Shakespeare 2006), fostered a view of disability as a dysfunction of the organism, something that could be cured only through sanitary interventions. In what follows, I will provide a brief history of the development of a political perspective on disability, to highlight the importance of political awareness over social environments and their value in promoting effective inclusionary tools. This inquiry will serve as a background to the analysis of an example of law inspired by capability-based policies, that will expose – *in actu* – the flaws of this model of inclusion.

During the 1970s, activists started a struggle to promote a social comprehension of disability, rejecting the "medical model" as an inadequate approach, one that considers the impact of structures, sites, relationships and policies (see e.g. Cremonesi 2012; Lettieri 2013). This alternative approach (usually labelled as "interactional" or "relational") includes a wide range of positions: from more conservative ones, in which individuals' impairments and medicalizing procedures still retain an important role in understanding and dealing with disability; to more radical ones, in which an understanding of disability as a personal condition is abandoned to embrace a view of social practices as imposing specific standards (a certain height, some basic capabilities, a specific mobility and so on) and thus nurturing differences.

Generally, all interactional approaches allow the identification of disability as an uneven situation intensified (if not created) by social structures and call for more appropriate policies and strategies to include non-standardized bodies and people with impairments.[7] Supporters of these approaches advocate the importance of "an analysis of the ways in which society actually disables [...] impaired people" (UPIAS 1975:12).[8] From this point of view, bodily impairments are

7 This point of view has been ratified by the United Nations Convention on the Rights of Persons with Disabilities: "Recognizing that disability is an evolving concept and that disability results from the interaction between persons with impairments and attitudinal and environmental barriers that hinders their full and effective participation in society on an equal basis with others." Available online at http://www.un.org/disabilities/default.asp?navid=13&pid=150 (last accessed October 2018).

8 As Tom Shakespeare (2006:19–25) explains, the expression "social model" is unequivocally linked to its English roots. See also Snyder and Mitchell (2006:5–11), where the authors confront the social model with a different, "milder" approach in which disability is seen as "a site of phenomenological value that is not purely synonymous with the processes of social disablement". Thus, it defines a precise tendency that cannot be overlaid to the huge variety of approaches that see disability as a question of social discrimination. One of the most significant features of the UK strand is the clear cut between social disability and subjective impairment: in many other

considered truly relevant only in relation to a (somehow externally and actively) limited access to social life. In treating disability as a problem that concerns individuals, governing institutions "divert [their] attention from the real problems [...] seeking its remedy in the opposite direction from the social cause by concentrating on the assessment of the individual" (UPIAS 1975:12).

Contrary to the medical approach to disability, interactional models promote the reorganization of public sites and social practices on the basis of more inclusive premises. Policies should be engaged in amending those (physical and virtual) sites of exclusion not by pursuing a forced integration into given standards, but rather by dismantling structures that reinforce the privileges of ableness. This paradigm finds its cornerstone in the understanding of disability as a "condition of disadvantage that originates in prejudices and modifiable social factors" (Zanichelli 2013:205, author's translation).

Once disability comes to be seen as a situation "caused by social conditions", old paradigms of care and help (that were basically centred on medicalization, internment and paternalistic projects of inclusion)[9] leave space for more complex and far-reaching solutions. The marginalization of people with disability "requires for its elimination" – in the words of the activists of the Union of the Physically Impaired Against Segregation (UPIAS), see UPIAS (1975:3)[10] –

> (a) that no one aspect such as incomes, mobility or institutions is treated in isolation, (b) that disabled people should, with the advice and help of others, assume control over their own lives, and (c) that professionals, experts and others who seek to help must be committed to promoting such control by disabled people.

The integrated approach supported by promoters of the interactional model calls upon policies to reshape the cultural, material, institutional environment and to supply disabled people and their families with tools and services aimed at encouraging an active and autonomous management of people's own lives.

---

traditions this separation is fuzzier. Since my goal here is not to trace a history of disability studies, I refer again to Shakespeare (2006) and Stiker (1999) for a complete exposition.

9 A similar shift has taken place in the debate on transgenderism. Medicalization is no longer seen as a "blessed" intervention that allows the subject to be integrated in everyday life. See Flavia Monceri's (2011:68 ff) reflections on the rejection of the authority of physicians and health workers and Pat Califia (2003) on hormonal treatment and surgery. The same unsettling position has been taken by feminists that challenge the role of gynaecologists; on this, see the issue on women's health *Donna Women Femme* 2015, Voll. 103–104. Particularly relevant are the so-called "labs" (such as "Gynepunk") in which women take on a form of shared and self-check-up, available online at http://www.dwf.it/gynepunk-lab-ginecologici-autonomi/ (last visited November 2018).

10 For a brief introduction to UPIAS, his goals and members, see again Shakespeare (2006:10–14). Here the author sheds light on the composition of the group, its goals and history and the reasons why UPIAS never grew "into a mass movement".

In the last decades, this perspective has been largely endorsed[11]: the recognition of the social origin of exclusion, and the related recognition that some people suffer marginalization not because of their impairments, but rather because of "something imposed on top of [their] impairments" (UPIAS 1975:3),[12] allows to identify people with disabilities as an oppressed social category, "unnecessarily isolated and excluded from full participation in society" (UPIAS 1975:3–4). Supporters of interactional models propose a political approach to disability which, in refusing the medical model and avoiding any unidirectional causal model, becomes able to identify new alternative paths to deal with impairments. Only by neglecting the understanding of impairment as a *medical* concern can the intervention upon bodies be reduced and a more sustainable and effective political strategy be adopted.

In its most radical inflections (see e.g. Kafer 2013; Kumari Campbell 2013; McRuer 2006; Sherry 2004), the interactional approach advocates non-assimilationist positions, in which disability is defined "as a site of resistance and a source of cultural agency previously suppressed" (Snyder and Mitchell 2006:10) and turns into a political platform for dissent.[13] Nonetheless, I want to focus here on a milder articulation of the interactional approach, one that draws on the capability model and has been largely applied in the organization of political interventions. This latter account explores the question of disability by balancing medical and social considerations of impairments. It entails an analysis of the social value of disability without forgetting the predicament of an impaired body, marked by objective personal difficulties. Tom Shakespeare (2006:61) offers a clear perspective of the premises of this political position when he observes that "impairment almost always plays some role in the lives of disabled people, even if social arrangements or cultural context minimizes the exclusion or disadvantage".[14] This approach involves the combination of both poles of the question,

11 As, for instance, the ratification of The Convention on the Rights of Persons with Disabilities in 2006 demonstrates. Here, it is clearly stated that "persons with disabilities [are to be viewed] as 'subjects' with rights, [...] capable of claiming those rights and making decisions for their lives based on their free and informed consent". Available online at http://www.un.org/disabilities/default.asp?navid=13&pid=150 (last accessed October 2018).

12 In this light, disability is intended as something caused by social factors (from individual – age, sex – to social ones – education, spaces, job opportunities), while the term "impairment" comes to signify a physical or mental status that differs from what is considered to be normal. This distinction is not accepted among advocates of radical interactional who understand impairment as something that has "both human variation encountering environmental obstacles and socially mediated difference that lends group identity and phenomenological perspective" (Snyder and Mitchell 2006:10). In this way, disability ceases to be marked "only [as] discriminatory encounters". An account of different terms (e.g. "physically impaired people", "disabled people", "mentally ill", "mentally handicapped") is outlined in Shakespeare (2006:11).

13 See, for instance, the debate on "transability": Arfini (2010, 2014), Stevens (2011). The issue has also been addressed by several newspapers and other media sources, see, among others, Boesveld (2015).

14 Far from being a provocation, it is possible to find several examples of the social construction of "objective impairments". In his research, Ian Hacking (1995b) displays the mechanism at work in such "making up" in the cases of schizophrenia, hysteria and MID, demonstrating the

propounding an understanding of disability as "a challenge" represented by "something that we might want to minimise but which we cannot ultimately avoid" (Shakespeare 2006:63). In examining the overlap of subjective troubles, environmental barriers and social obstacles, such an approach casts a different light on disability. In this sense, it draws its main stance from the capability approach: the concern for an adjustment of the social background (which could be described as the guarantee of secured capabilities) is always contingent on the idea that some functionings should be developed in order to take part in a political community.

While a mild relational strategy might put forward effective solutions for changing the situation of disabled people, by addressing both their personal situation (e.g. by providing services of day care) and enhancing their participation in public activity (e.g. by creating accessible areas), it also entails potential backlashes. By recognizing functionings as the basis of any political participation, capability-based policies that implement a mild relational strategy risk not only excluding, but actually erasing people who do not fulfil minimum standards of normality. Capabilities-based policies reveal their worse pitfalls when it comes to accounting for those people who do not match the list of features intended as necessary to be considered as active members of the political community. Based on this analysis, I will take into account some cases of capability-based policies applied to disability in order to highlight some main flaws of this approach.

Public policies and legal norms addressed to people with disability take a variety of shapes: many things are left to civil society organizations (such as voluntary associations and churches and, above all, self-organized families or caregivers), while state's support usually comes under the form of subsidies or foundations for maintaining civil society organizations. These funds are usually juxtaposed to dedicated spaces for the disabled and the guarantee of job, education and opportunities of civic engagement. Interventions aim at providing a wide range of opportunities for those who lack, permanently or temporarily, the possibility of taking part in everyday activities. Based on this, it is possible to imagine capabilities-based policies as the equivalent of ramps: as ramps adjust the environment to non-average needs and provide a substitutive way to reach the bottom of the stairs without climbing them, so do capabilities-based policies pave the way for reaching a given point, that is, a "normal" objective or achievement to which each and every one has the right to aspire. To put it another way, the strategy adopted promotes the achievement of common widespread standards while arranging them differently. By encouraging "sameness-in-difference", capability-based policies force people with special needs and non-average skills both to strive for obtaining goals, which are arbitrary but have taken on the status of natural aspirations, and to undertake a special path in order to achieve

common root of these disturbances and the high degree of artificiality they share. A narrower – and more astonishing – case is the rising of the Attention Deficit Hyperactivity Disorder, a quite young syndrome (in this vest, it is less than 100 years), with a huge incidence that entails very heavy treatments.

such common goals. In the discrepancy between the (variable) means and the (unified) targets, unfair conditions at several levels come to be established. It is possible to find out to what extent the lives of people with disability are influenced by such a bifurcation by examining different macro-areas of life, such as mobility and the overall relation with one's own environment; the degree of engagement in ordinary everyday activity; and, finally, the prospect of living an adult life (which usually entails both financial autonomy, usually determined by job opportunities, and an emotional autonomy, usually actualized in the possibility of choosing one's own sentimental relations).

For what concerns the issues of mobility and the relation with the environment, the differentiation of spaces and everyday activities might constitute a great burden for people with disability. Far from promoting integration, the constitution of dedicated areas in which people with certain impairments can experience a world tailored to their needs keeps them captive in a condition of social exclusion by creating enclosures and lowering real opportunities of participation.[15] Similarly, the creation of communities of people with disability might become a subtle form of segregation.[16] In this sense, too often do state institutions and private/semi-private organizations enact a debilitating process both on subjects themselves and on their caregivers and families by creating parallel social groups and sustaining the value of such a disorienting experience of the environment, social dynamics and affective relationships.[17] The implementation of diversified structures for containing people with disability can take many shapes.

The aforementioned differentiation can be traced even in the material, physical conformation of urban spaces. Barriers and frontiers, confines and borders, customs and obstacles are part of our social daily life and we are used to dealing with these phenomena. As many theorists have demonstrated, the organization of metropolis and cities (Castells 1972; Secchi 2013) as well as the architecture of houses and their internal divisions (McRuer 2006; Preciado 2014) convey strong messages and influence those who inhabit them and their (spatial and non-spatial) horizons.

By looking at the organization of cities and metropolises it is possible to draw a social topography of groups and populations that inhabit urban spaces (Secchi 2013; Secchi and Viganò 2009). Such a lively map displays not only the growth of the city, but also

15 Indeed, I am not denying the crucial importance of services, such as ramps or blind trails, elevators or dedicated toilets. Nonetheless, it is precisely in the organization of spaces (where to allocate services) that a "city of impaired" is mapped out. The establishment of a "free zone" available to everybody determines (*ex negativo*) forbidden areas. See Kafer (2013).

16 I am not speaking here of self-organized communities, as I am more concerned with spaces expressly created for assisting people with disability (or marginalized people *tout court*).

17 A hint of this Janus-faced integration can be grasped by looking at the formula "*diversamente abile*", literally "differently able", the polite way used in Italy to refer to disabled and handicapped people. This locution conveys the sense of a compulsory normality that must be pursued, though the subject cannot achieve certain standards. This expression, then, denies the possibility of a radical difference, in which different criteria should be applied.

> the social inequalities and the way in which these inequalities give life to glaring forms of spatial unfairness, together with the outcomes of climate change and the problems connected to a conception of mobility as forming part of citizenship rights. (Secchi 2013:6; author's translation)

Which is to say, urban structures speak to a vast history and represent the scenario of an ongoing transformation, in which social, political and individual plans are intertwined. Similarly, domestic spaces have been "reinvented" as "social workshop for the making of *men*" (Goodrich in McRuer 2006:91, emphasis added). Houses and flats exhibit standards of living that "not only maintained a strict gendered division of labour (which simultaneously nurtured the new heterosexual identities and intimacies)"[18] and "opposed the orderly, managed home to the [...] unruly, disordered homes" of wretched people, but also established the private realm "as a primary site for consumption" (McRuer 2006:91). Places structured around able-bodied, heterosexual, private values contribute to transforming the alternative body in an impaired one. The body itself becomes the obstacle that hampers access, while the creation of "institutional locations" for people with disability yields "debilitating effects through taxonomies of naming, the statistical calculation of average and nonstandard bodies, restrictive public policy implementation, and especially participation in a normative science of eugenic origin" (Snyder and Mitchell 2006:5).

In negotiating spaces of the urban context and the domestic arrangements, individuals are bargaining their involvement in the public sphere, that is, their own citizenship and their private reality, along with their possible connections and relations. It is important to stress two features of this condition of restraint. First, a limited access to physical public spaces causes a remarkable weakening of one's political identity, since it is also anchored to shared experiences of common reality. Civic isolation is, thus, produced by obstructing autonomous choices in ways that render certain places structurally inaccessible for certain people. This physical arrangement takes the shape of a tangible and material "naturalization of citizenship rights".[19] Moreover, on an individual basis, this limitation results in the impossibility of enjoying a web of fruitful social and affective relationships. Being excluded from intrapersonal connections thwarts the opportunity of forming spontaneous groups. Moreover, it enhances segregation of discriminated subjects by lowering the circumstances, spaces and events for people with disability to get in touch with diverse people. This is the way in which all marginalized groups are compulsively dismembered and kept divided by the dismantling of melting pots, which ends up confining certain realities to

18 See also Preciado (2014).

19 It is a process in which political belonging is subsumed under (and prejudiced by) "nature", that is, by biological features which reach a political status. In this sense, too often being a woman, being a child, having a disability, being a refugee, having a non-heterosexual orientation have an impact on one's value in the social realm.

particular realms. As Tamar Pitch (2013) nicely explains,[20] one of the ways in which this form of segregation is produced in public spaces is the pursuing of an idea of *decency.* Interventions of revaluation aim at increasing urban decorum by cleaning, expelling dissonant elements. Parallel to the relocation of garbage in dumps, "human wastes" are exposed to the ill-placed interventions imposed from above and meant to restore decency. The control of the space is nothing but an amplification of the control of bodies: as in the case of the Schengen Area (see Sossi 2006), where a widespread control of the individuals goes hand in hand with a harsh limitation of spaces and access, marginalization is performed by an active banishment from "decorous" areas and by an isolation of singular individuals. If this is true for all kinds of discrimination, people with disability are much more affected by bodily bounds. In a condition of impairment, subjects experience both a limited mobility and a bumpy interaction with architectural barriers. In being "not geographically invariant" (Imrie 2000:21), people with disability succumb under the burden of segregation, to the extent that this status of seclusion comes to be interiorized and accepted as inevitable.

The "spatiality of disability" has its central trait in the *obstacle.* Like in a reversed map, it displays the series of impossible places, obstructed paths, unattainable venues. The sense of marginalization is strengthened by the creation of discrete zones, which become accessible ghettos for the disabled. Such zones do not take the form of public squares or melting pots but are conceived as reserved spaces tailored to a specific type of costumers. From asylums and day-care centres to special schools and public transports, people with disability are not only isolated from social activities and intercourses, but are trapped in a net of institutions that aim to "discipline, protect and/or control [...] all of which serve to demarcate and segregate disabled people" (Imrie 2000:7).

The case of spatiality offers a very clear idea of the predicament constituted by having an impairment, and, at the same time, highlights the pragmatic flaws of a system based on the postulation of standards rather than on a broader reimagining of the present. In fact, it casts light on a very tough condition: external structures determine what kind of life a disabled can aspire to. Architectonical barriers, urban settings and discrete places built for people with disability constitute the two faces of a milieu that encloses and controls the entire horizon of the disabled experience. Space represents the physical validation of a process of disempowerment that works all along disabled lives. It forces people with disability to rely on other people for help and choices, in a loop of dependency that permeates all the dimensions of disabled daily reality. Physical borders, in fact, stand out as an inhibition of one's own autonomy: not only limiting the possibility of movement and control over one's planning, but also imposing the constant supervision of third parties in order for a disabled to reach places and go through

20 Note that Pitch's reflection touches upon a wider range of discriminated groups and is particularly interested in those groups considered "harmful" for public decency, such as prostitutes or people who are addicted to drugs/people who sell drugs.

the city. In this way, the spatial organization of the city (what would be intended as the most material expression of a political rationality) is characterized by the manifest incapacity of dismantling embodied dynamics of disempowerment.

Another, though less tangible, structure that connotes the experience of people with disability is the everyday routine that they are invited to follow. By looking into the example of day-care centres, we can get a privileged perspective for the observation of compulsory procedures that structure the everyday lives of people with disability that are doomed incapable of working. Associations of volunteers promoting activities for physically and mentally impaired people offer didactic laboratories (theatre groups, music, choruses, gardening and others), or activities based on a one-to-one relationship. They aim at encouraging socialization of disabled people and their inclusion in the public sphere. Nonetheless, these associations constitute a very feeble link between disabled people and society at large. In being conceived as protected spaces, these institutions are more akin to private clubs or asylums than to convivial realities. Moreover, these are usually characterized by a strong hierarchical structure, in which caregivers and care-receivers are clearly separated from each other. In this division, differences are reinforced and isolation is reinstated once again as the main feature of some people's experience. People with disabilities are perceived in these contexts as service users. By spending most of their time with therapists or support workers, their possibility of interlacing equal relation decreases dramatically. Interactions are mostly shaped as vertical ones, and this plays as a severe limitation for psychical/emotional development. Indeed, discrepancy becomes particularly alarming in the case of children, in that by being "always accompanied by adults they are denied access to the social world of children, and they may be unable to take part in age-appropriate activities and express the typical resistance of children and young people" (Shakespeare 2006:171).

The binary division disabled/able ends up being a totalizing categorization supported by hierarchical structures and patterns of action, so as to reinforce biases that will performatively operate in broader social interactions, with the consequence that "[m]any disabled people are in the community, but not part of the community" (Shakespeare 2006:174). A good hint at this situation is provided by the report written by Eileen Hyder and Cathy Tissot (2013:3–4) about their examination of reactions and impressions of blind women and men who take part in library-reading groups. The organization of discrete reading groups in British libraries, modelled on the demands of participants, might seem to be beneficial to blind people, but the interviews conducted by the authors revealed a general discontent among participants. They were mainly concerned with "feeling excluded as a reader" and express doubts about "the role of the group in supporting reading, and the role of the librarian in facilitating the group" (Hyder and Tissot 2013:4). The composition of the group was the first obstacle: as it was only addressed to blind people, the reading experience became a further moment of segregation. Although it permitted a deeper, worthwhile analysis of shared conditions (e.g. blindness, Hyder and Tissot 2013:7), it also reinforced the awareness of a characteristic that does not allow being considered a "normal" reader. This awareness was aggravated by the scarcity of books at the disposal of blind people. Participants complained about the quality of material supports provided for them and the quantity of titles available. On the one hand, not everyone was able to read braille and all other types of support had flaws. Moreover, as observed by one of the group members, while most of the books available for blind readers were published for commercial interests and had huge costs, the ones made with "charitable" purposes were too often very low-quality products.[21] On the other hand, limited choice and the impossibility of picking but some titles worsen the isolation of blind readers, in relation to non-blind ones.[22] In addition, the position of the librarian generated more controversies. Librarians emerged more as leaders than as hosts: they took most of the decisions about the organization without involving readers. The "facilitation" of the group's activity performed by the librarian put the participants in a situation of passive acceptance of imposed choices. Not only bodily or economic factors conditioned their experiences as readers, but the whole organization was inclined to conceive them more as disabled than as readers.

The situation worsens when the typical structure that has been described above is assimilated by, and embedded in, the law. Regulations can in fact strengthen social habits by imposing them from above. Policies drafted on the basis of a knowledge that too often objectifies and homogenize the experience of disabled people complicate their social condition. The case of Italian norms on disability illustrates how having access to public funds is linked to the fulfilment of some very strict requirements, which often forces caregivers and family members of disabled people to deceive social workers (see Onnis 2013). Practices and policies blossom under the form of answers to contingent problems or remedies to abstract predicaments. The public rhetoric on disabled and not-autonomous people is sublimated into norms and laws too often incapable of meeting real needs of real individuals and their families.

Italian norms on disability and discrimination are aimed at regulating social integration of people with disability and countering discrimination[23] by the

21 For a broader discussion on the issue of charity, see Shakespeare (2006:153–165).

22 As Jane, an interviewee aged 50, blind since childhood, remarked, the impossibility to avail herself of a reasonable range of books where she might get recently published books entailed "peer pressure [...] because everybody else is reading it, you feel you should be part of it" (Hyder and Tissot 2013:8).

23 Pivotal in this sense is L. 104/1992, which reads:

> Art. 1 purpose: 1. The Republic: a. guarantees full respect for human dignity and the rights of freedom and autonomy of the handicapped person and promotes their full integration in the family, school, at work and in society; b. prevents and removes the disabling conditions that prevent the development of the human person, to achieve the maximum possible autonomy and participation of disabled persons in community life, as well as the realization of civil, political and financial; c. pursues the functional and social recovery of the person affected by physical, psychic and sensory, and securing the services and benefits for the prevention, care and rehabilitation of disabilities, as well as the legal protection and economic handicapped person; d. predisposes interventions aimed at overcoming of alienation and

means of subsidies as well as by the organization of educational and working sessions or the provision of benefits for families and caregivers:

> Although a remarkable gap remains between the declarations of rights and their actualization, with the emergence of welfare and the principle of substantial equality the law has taken a key role as a means to social inclusion of disabled people: legal orders guarantee equal opportunities in their favoring and prohibiting any discrimination to their disadvantage. (Zanichelli 2013:206)[24]

Italian L. n. 104/1992 is an interesting instance to begin with in order to see the concealed effects under these manifest aims. The spirit of the law is to give disabled people and their significant others the possibility of living a good life and having a smooth relation with their environment, and aims at guaranteeing basic human rights. It reads:

> Art. 4. The exercise of the right to education cannot be prevented by learning difficulties or other difficulties originating from disability-related impairments.

In order to guarantee this right, the law specifies that:

> Art. 5. The identification of the student as disabled person and the acquisition of documents related to the functional diagnosis is accompanied by a dynamic functional profile meant to produce an individualized educational plan, which is jointly formulated with the cooperation of the parents of the disabled person, the local heath operators and [...] the teaching body [...]. The profile indicates the physical, psychical, social and relational characteristics of the student, and highlights both the learning difficulties [...] and the skills that have to be supported, enhanced and progressively reinforced and developed in accordance with the cultural choices of the disabled person.

After having established the "dynamic functional profile" of the student with disability, scholastic institutions and teachers must accompany the pupil in a customized career. This does not mean that schools or special programmes/procedures for the disabled have to be provided, because L. 104/1992 art. 12, clause 3 clearly states that disabled people have to be *integrated* in schools. Given that, schools must have adequate structures and qualified personnel to provide a valuable educational experience to children with disability. To fulfil these requirements, institutions need money in order to hire people and properly

social exclusion of the handicapped person. (author's translation); the original text is available online at http://www.normattiva.it/uri-res/N2Ls?urn:nir:stato:legge:1992-02-05;104!vig= (last accessed October 2018).

24 For a reflection of policies on disability in US and EU, see Zanichelli (2013).

arrange spaces. Moreover, there is no mention of a maximum number of disabled students that can be accommodated in a classroom.[25] In this sense, the spirit of the law is completely respected. But what real families, teachers and student do experience is unbearable. The problem of integration is here intertwined with economic, social and material possibilities, as well as with the need for the school to comply with standards of profit.

It is glaring that standards that art. 4 of L. 104/1998 set are *impossible* to be met for certain people[26]: children affected by strong impairments (as in the case of the so called "pillow angels") cannot take advantage of participating in activities from which they are *structurally* excluded, because of a lack of skills and a particular conformation that do not match the required standards. In much the same way, the EU directive n. 2000/78 on "establishing a general framework for equal treatment in employment and occupation" show same type of weaknesses. While it "stress[es] the need to foster a labour market favourable to social integration by formulating a coherent set of policies aimed at combating discrimination against groups such as persons with disability" and establishes that "[e]mployment and occupation are key elements in guaranteeing equal opportunities for all and contribute strongly to the full participation of citizens in economic, cultural and social life and in realising their potential",[27] it also states:

> Art. 17 – This Directive does not require the recruitment, promotion, maintenance in employment or training of an individual who is not competent, capable and available to perform the essential functions of the post concerned or to undergo the relevant training, without prejudice to the obligation to provide reasonable accommodation for people with disabilities.

Needless to say, no companies are called upon to accommodate people who are not suitable for the job, but then the pitfall of this system comes to surface again. In the implementation of policies aimed at fostering the development of allegedly shared skills, a huge gap separates those who are deprived of such skills and imprison them into a new form of marginalization, which seems impossible to overcome.

25 On the contrary, the number of foreign students is regulated. Despite art. 45 of the DPR 349/1999 which requires that foreign students must not exceed the number of Italian students per class, the circular n. 101/2010 sets the limit to 30% of the total students in a classroom. The decision was taken in order to not slow down the progresses of Italian students, see available online at http://www.tuttoscuola.com/portali/iscrizioniscolastiche/archivio-24581.html (last accessed November 2018).

26 Interesting commentaries on rehabilitation and processes aimed to get disabled people to obtain average capabilities or functionings can be found in Mitchell and Snyder (2000), Stiker (1999), Shakespeare (2006).

27 Council Directive 2000/78/EC of 27 November 2000 establishing a general framework for equal treatment in employment and occupation, art. 8 and 9. It is available online at http://eur-lex.europa.eu/LexUriServ/LexUriServ.do?uri=CELEX:32000L0078:en:HTML (last accessed November 2018).

3 Model 3

Category-protecting policies

This chapter sets out to examine the class of policies that I dubbed *category-protecting*. As the name suggests, this type of inclusive policies aspires to improve the conditions of marginalized individuals and groups by providing a set of legal instruments aimed at protecting them or improving their life conditions. These policies operate through the discouragement of behaviours that are deemed to be detrimental to marginalized individuals or by extending existing rights to people who belong to marginalized groups. Therefore, in the category-protecting model, the path towards inclusion is no longer conceived as the top-down endowment of opportunities (whether at political or personal level). Rather, inclusion is deeply connected with the recognition of categories of people who need to be legally protected or supported. In this approach, recognition is the ultimate feature of inclusion, since it allows to become visible, to retain a sociopolitical identity and thus a well-defined position. Recognition plays out as an enablement, a sort of liberation through legitimation.

As the name suggests, then, category-protecting policies are contingent on processes of recognition. The legislator is called upon to map the social sphere in search for emergent groups whose members are marginalized on the grounds of specific conducts or belongings. This form of recognition is contingent on the existence of homogeneous social groups, whose members share specific kinds of traits.[1] This reading leads to an understanding of the social world as a patchwork of different, discrete categories that encompass or label single subjects. In being legally treated as a category member, the subject of law is no longer unique, but comes to be defined in accordance with those features that qualify an individual's social identity.

While the opportunity-oriented model and the capability-based one were respectively premised on the political or philosophical definition of a subject of law, this model builds his subjects on significant features which emerge out of an evaluation of social behaviours and roles. This entails that the legal recognition

1 I would like to remark that it is very unusual to describe someone as "heterosexual". For, the mark always specifies a distance from the norm. In indicating the difference, the mark stigmatizes, see Burke et al. (2000), Goffman (1963), Guaraldo (2015), Haslanger 2012, Livia et al. (1997), McConnel-Ginet (2003).

of a subject is always related to her being socially recognized, which in turn is linked to the endorsement and the re-enactment of standardized and accepted identity features. Unsurprisingly, the subject to which category-protecting policies are addressed is very different from the one presupposed by the policies I examined earlier in this work. Both opportunity-oriented and capability-based strategies consider the subject of law to be an individual as a unit. Whether abstract or highly determined in her traits, the subject taken into account is regarded as pre-constituted either as a citizen or as a human being. As we have seen, these legal subjects rely on pregiven categorization. This means that they can be neither entirely created nor entirely revoked by legal recognition.

Interestingly, the relation between social and legal recognition is a two-way one. While policymakers cannot but rely on already accepted identity categories, legal ratification of social categories reinforces and somehow modifies the way in which these identity groups are perceived. The conferral of a legal recognition not only gives categories a higher stability and visibility, but at the same time perimeters the limits of intelligibility. This twofold recognition and the consequent interaction between social and legal visibility set in motion a powerful mechanism of naturalization that tends to conceal the arbitrariness and the social constructedness of the categories themselves to the point that behaviours, habits and a whole range of personal features end up being perceived as inborn in the very nature of certain identities. They become standardized characteristics of crystallized categories. Showing certain attitudes, therefore, not only opens up the way to be legally recognized, but also becomes key to acquiring a social position within the political community.

However, the circular interaction between this two-way type of recognition and the naturalization of identity categories significantly impacts on social organization, identity formation and finally the understanding of inclusion. Marginalization and inclusion are in fact reshaped accordingly to what turns out to be politically relevant in the eyes of the law. This does not mean that marginalization is a thoroughly made-up phenomenon. Rather, what I am suggesting is that certain forms of marginalization come to be accounted in a specific way due to the formation of *a body of knowledge around them*. Based on that, the relation between the recognized subjects and the law takes the form of a dynamic interplay in which the two poles influence and alter each other.

In reading the social realm as a conglomerate of groups, category-protecting policies pursue what I will portray as a paradoxical objective. They advocate the implementation of policy measures designed to tackle a kind of exclusion that originates from an objectified and seemingly inseparable connection between a subject's identity and the category she belongs to. In being posed by the law, and hence, in becoming the main path to access rights and privileges guaranteed by the law, this connection is invoked and reinforced by the recognized subjects themselves. Both in the enactment of protective measures and in the extension of rights, this type of policies relies on people's self-ascription to identity categories. This is evidence of the high degree of co-dependence between the legal delineation of a category and its social imposition: extending benefits to, and safeguarding, certain categories means prompting people to articulate their condition following notions and categories embedded in the law.

Category-protecting policies, in this sense, indicate legal recognition as the basic measure against marginalization. However, as I have already mentioned, this type of legal recognition comes under two guises: the extension of existing rights for disadvantaged groups and the containment of discriminatory conducts.

In the first case, category-protecting policies issue recognition through the extension of existing rights to disadvantaged groups. Instances of this approach can be found in the extension of marital rights to same-sex couples or in norms concerning adoption for LGBT or single people. In these cases, the legislator endows with existing rights some categories that were not benefitting from specific privileges due to a lack of legal recognition. This kind of law operates along the lines of similarity: the legislator institutes a correspondence among different relationships on the ground of shared distinctive traits. Indeed, it is up to the legislator to *decide* which features are relevant to fall under the scope of the law. The extension of marital rights to same-sex couples, for instance, keeps the requirement of coupledom while rejecting the idea that the couple has to be formed by a woman and a man. In this way, marriage is reframed around some of its essential traits to allow the legitimation of nonconforming affective relationships. More in general, inclusion is achieved by adjusting an obsolete legal body to alternative ways of living, that come to be encompassed in a traditional matrix (see Butler and Athanasiou 2013, Butler and Venditti 2014, Venditti 2019).

In the second case, category-protecting policies take the form of provisions for physical protection (e.g. in the case of "pentiti")[2] as well as of safeguarding procedures for victims of harassment (e.g. in the case of homophobic behaviours and hate speech). Alternatively, they can provide for various types of assistance for vulnerable categories.[3] For instance, they might result in laws designed to

2 *Pentito* (plur. "pentiti") is the term for designating those people who used to be members of criminal organizations and during their imprisonment decide to facilitate investigations by sharing information about crucial events and the organization itself. This figure is sanctioned in the Italian legislation in L. n. 82/1991. Despite the appearances, the category of *pentiti* mirrors the other categories that require protection. Legal protection is not contingent on the "goodness" of the participants to the category. It is worth noting that protection is issued for contrasting social discrimination and does not entail a *moral* assessment of the reasons lying behind discrimination itself. The figure of the "pentito" is exemplar: at the very moment a former participant of a criminal organization (such as *Mafia* or other hierarchical and enclosed groups) decides to "renege" its community of belonging (which is actually a parallel community to the body politic), he is rejected from his community. This specific policy of inclusion is not an assessment of the reasons that have led to exclusion, but rather a cluster of strategic political measures that aim at the re-composition of a unitary social community.

3 I would like to mention that also some types of female quotas or specific laws concerning women fall into the category-protecting policies. A distinction should be made between policies that aim at creating *equal* opportunities for women (and thus extending "manly" possibilities to women, so that both genders get – at least in theory – equal possibilities in the public sector) and policies that offer a set of gender-specific safeguards/endowments applicable to the private or/and the public spheres. The latter's goal is not to *level* women's status vis-à-vis men's one (which is

promote more flexible working time arrangements for mothers or caretakers, in specific measures to assist the victims of cybercrimes[4] or other vulnerable categories. These measures are not simply meant to delineate an effective way to support disadvantaged subjects. Rather, category-protecting policies aspire to identify and address the root cause of discrimination related to the violence against people on the basis of their specific identity or individual preferences. The legislator is called upon identifying pockets of marginalization to make them legally ***visible***. Their objective is not so much restricted to the provision of protection, as it concerns the achievement of a widespread recognition for those conducts and forms of life that are socially targeted as nonconforming and thus subjected to social stigma.

On this account, inclusion which is no longer regarded as the possibility for a single subject to be legally involved in social interactions (which might eventuate in the ineffective, occasional attempt to reintegrate single individuals), indeed is understood as a more complex process of integration of diverse realities into the social world. The law turns a social stigma into an asylum and transmutes its social meaning by authoritatively recognizing nonconforming conducts or alternative forms of protection and respect.

It is possible to see these measures at work in anti-discriminatory bills against gender-related violence or, more in general, against hate speech. The debate over the extension of the current Italian legislation on discrimination might offer a good example of the shape legal recognition takes within the scope of category-protecting policies. This example illustrates the path from social to legal recognition in such a way as to highlight what can be considered as ***the constitution of a legitimated stigmatization***.

In 2013, after a spate of violent acts against LGBT people in Italy,[5] more than 200 MPs led by Ivan Scalfarotto promoted the extension of the Italian law on discrimination (L. n. 205/1993, commonly referred to as *Legge Mancino*) in such a way that homophobic behaviours be legally repressed.[6] Originally, the

considered to be the standard one), but to provide a wider set of rights in order to prevent unfair situations. An example of the first type of female quotas can be the acquisition of rights formerly considered to be men's prerogatives (such as the right to vote, the possibility of joining the army and so on), while the second type comprises financial assistance for female entrepreneurs as well as definite forms of protection from gender-related crimes (as stalking, abuses, mobbing, etc.).

4 Revenge porn concerns the circulation of "porn" materials (pictures, videos) posted online by victims' ex-partners. Until 2012, it was almost impossible to sue perpetrators because there was no legal fact-type under which to subsume the crime. Indeed, victims (above all girls) are neither stalked, nor threatened, nor injured, nor wounded. They cannot accuse websites owners, who are not responsible for what third parties upload on their websites. In the US they cannot even charge their ex-boyfriends because of the First Amendment and the protection of free speech (see Goode 2013).

5 See the report by Amnesty International available online at http://www.amnesty.it/Italia-nuova-ondata-attacchi-omofobi-necessari-interventi-sul-piano-legislativo (last accessed on 25 October 2018).

6 Italy does not have a specific regulation against hate speech, but the issue of verbal and physical discrimination is regulated by L. 25 Giugno 1993, n. 205 in materia di "Conversione in legge,

Legge Mancino was explicitly aimed at contrasting social activities carried out by fascist organizations or, more generally, by groups or parties who "incite to perform or perpetrate discriminatory acts on racial, ethnic, national or religious grounds".[7] As the law stood, the legislator's intention is to restrain and sanction socially detrimental behaviours. Quite surprisingly, though, the amendment presented in March 2013 seemed to neglect this very focus to the advantage of a different understanding of the original target of the legal text. As the speech addressed to the Parliament on the 15th of March 2013 emphasizes, the main goal of the amendment was not to provide a stricter application of the law in terms of punishment, nor was it to add a clause of aggravation for those who act with discriminatory intents towards homosexual and/or transsexual people or "gender minorities" more generally. Rather, the amendment's chief goal was to recognize and ratify a minority who suffers from a systematic discrimination contingent on the identity of the members of the group itself. In other words, by sanctioning the systematic tie that connects certain types of offending acts to sex, gender and sexual choices, the amendment aimed first and foremost at identifying (and thus formally recognizing) the vulnerable status of people engaged in nonconforming sexual practices and relationships. The premise to the proposal presented to the Chamber of Deputies discloses this tendency:

> In homophobic and transphobic harassment and discrimination, the specificity of the sexual orientation of the victim, as well as their *being homosexual or transsexual*, or their *being a woman* (in the context, for instance, of sexual assault) are not neutral with respect to the crime itself. [Such identity features] *constitute the grounds, the reasons and, technically speaking, the motive of the crime.* Nor is the author of the offense neutral on these respects, since they feel contempt and hatred for *the victim themselves.*[8]

The opening sentence of the proposal precisely refers to a subjective condition that "causes" or "triggers" the offense. In this sense, the question of discriminatory behaviours has not to be couched in terms of a violation of human rights or of a "general" inequitable attitude. It has to be championed as deriving from a prejudiced and offensive approach to certain ways of living. Scalfarotto and the other signatories of the amendment advocated *the inclusion of a fact-type* to the ones that the law originally encompassed. Such an amendment was presented not as an operation on the essence of the law (whose main goal, once again, was to punish incitement to discriminatory behaviours), which remained untouched. It was rather conceived as a push for the *legal identification of a further*

---

con modificazioni, del decreto-legge 26 aprile 1993, n. 122, recante misure urgenti in materia di discriminazione razziale, etnica e religiosa".

7 Author's translation. The original text is available online at http://www.normattiva.it/uri-res/N2Ls?urn:nir:stato:decreto.legge:1993-04-26;122!vig= (last accessed on 25 October 2018).

8 Author's translation, emphasis added. The original is available online at http://www.camera.it/_dati/leg17/lavori/stampati/pdf/17PDL0003090.pdf (last accessed on 25 October 2018).

marginalized category. It is striking that the interest of the MPs did not lie in the enforcement of strict sanctions, as they urged a formal recognition of an alternative way of living and the consequent supply of protection for those who embrace it.

More precisely, leaving aside formal corrections or modifications regarding the main structure of the Act, the request submitted to the Parliament asked for an extension of the legislative instrument with an eye to recognize a further category as being in danger of discrimination. Nonetheless, as the parliamentary body required to assess the law (the Commissione Permanente Affari Costituzionali, Presidenza del Consiglio e degli Interni – hereinafter Commissione Permanente) stressed, this "new" category differs remarkably from the ones already encompassed by the Act. In fact, the features indicated in the Legge Mancino as possible grounds for discriminatory behaviours are related to something that goes beyond what can be considered as an individual preference.[9] Ethnicity, religion, nationality and race are determined by social or "natural" ties and/or denote a cultural belonging. This makes it difficult to liken these affiliations to homosexuality (as well as to all those behaviours which are technically considered as "gender dysphoric"),[10] given that the amendment both portrays sexual preferences as strongly connoted and univocally identifiable, and seems to take the biological/genetic origin of sexuality for granted. Much as neither the former nor the latter were purposely and explicitly put forward in the proposal, they are easily inferable from a careful reading of the text of the amendment.

The need for a sharper definition of the categories to which the amendment is addressed is an obstacle that generally concerns any extension of protective laws to heterogeneous groups. However, it turns out to be particularly intense in the demarcation of sexual minority groups. The anti-homophobia act addresses a vast number of cases, running from women and homosexuals to transgender people. Moreover, it does not delimit that which has to be included under the label "sexual minorities" – to the extent that women are still considered to fall under this categorization.[11] The problem of a lack of clarity in the proposal was

9 The report reads: "[W]hat has been established [by the amendment] can prefigure a normatively differentiated situation with respect to other situations that similarly deserve to be safeguarded, in which the crime is committed on the basis of personal conditions, so as to violate the principle of equality before the law". Author's translation. The original text is available online at http://www.camera.it/_dati/leg17/lavori/schedela/apriTelecomando_wai.asp?codice=17PDL0008650 (last accessed on 25 October 2018).

10 Here lies another ambiguity of the amendment, since its promoters claim it is issued against homophobia, whereas in the text a vast variety of "sexual minorities" are indicated (such as transvestisms, cross-dressing or transsexuality). Such an ambiguity poses a challenge to commentators since, in its fuzziness, the amendment indirectly promotes two discrete objectives. My understanding of the amendment and the prominence accorded to "homophobia" reflects a typical tendency of the Italian debate, where that topic was of paramount importance and obscured the other points touched upon by the proposal.

11 Note that, by including women, the very instability of other traits of gender dysphoria, reported by Commissione Permanente, drops.

pointed out in the report of the Commissione Permanente. Its members expressed scepticism about the possibility of incorporating in the law a broad and blurry group of people, whose characteristics remain, to say the least, inconsistent and underdefined. Who is to be protected? What are the crucial features for one to *become*, in the eyes of the law, a *vulnerable subject*? The amendment did not satisfy the constitutional requirement of "legal certainty", since it was referred to "wide and indeterminate situations and circumstances".[12] Furthermore, even if a more precise description could be provided, a thorny problem would persist, in that the conditions for belonging to such a protected group "are based on subjective choices (rather than on objective positions), which are in turn related to the sphere of individual wills, potentially unstable over time and therefore difficult to ascertain".[13] In highlighting the fuzziness of the considered category and its instability, the Commissione Permanente explicitly called for a twofold revision involving the need for a more precise definition of the gendered body that had to be protected and the indication of an invariable identity, whose steadiness might secure the legitimacy of recourse to the law. These remarks entailed the revision of the amendment in the light of legal certainty, as both required the creation of standards that would allow an evaluation and the consistent application of the law.[14] The legislator was formally asked to operate an abstraction and produce an image of the disadvantaged subject by embedding in the law a cluster of features useful for a straightforward and long-lasting identification of the people who might have recourse to the law.

The fulfilment of the demand for legal certainty was directly connected with the second obstacle that the Commissione Permanente identified. In fact, to accommodate the concerns of the Commissione Permanente, the legislator would have been forced to set forth an "adequate" description of the subject of law. But to be legally "adequate", a description must be coherent and stable, with the risk of introducing a substantive and naturalized account of sexuality. Insofar as legal certainty presupposes the establishment of stable standards, the legislator would have been asked to identify essential, non-contingent traits and ground its analysis on them. In other words, to find a place in the legal system, homosexuality should be integrated in it with a view to what is already conforming to legal procedures. In the case of Scalfarotto's amendment, for instance, homosexuality

12 The problem of setting boundaries and defining minority groups in a clear way has forever been an obstacle to the legal recognition of rights for the LGBT community; see, for instance, Gamson (1995:401).

13 Author's translation. The text continues by saying: "[The amendment has] for object inner motives which cannot be univocally and objectively assessed, may give rise to the presumption of subsistence whenever the felony is issued against a subject whose homosexuality or transsexuality are known, so as to introduce a reversal of the burden of proof". The original text is available online at http://www.camera.it/_dati/leg17/lavori/schedela/apriTelecomando_wai.asp?codice=17PDL0008650 (last accessed on 25 October 2018).

14 As a matter of fact, the Commissione Permanente declared that the ambiguity in the definition of the group would have made the amended law hardly enforceable, but – as many commentators contended – this could have also served the purpose of a broader inclusion.

should have been profiled as or rendered coherent to categories such as ethnicity, religion and nationality.[15] It would have had to take the form of an indelible mark that saturates the whole identity by constituting and regulating it. This means that in order for homosexuality and nonconforming gendered traits to be included in the legal text, they *have to* acquire the status of essential traits, entrenched in nature and determined by it.[16]

Moreover, categories embedded in the law should also prove consistent with general social expectations. To craft a category and draw a coherent classification, the legislator is called upon gathering a cluster of information concerning socially recognized forms of living. Social categories are carved out on the basis of empirical and scientific knowledge. These two types of knowledge represent the "fundamental codes of a culture". The former is composed by codes "governing its language, its schemas of perception, its exchanges, its techniques, its values, the hierarchy of its practices". These are "establish[ed] for every man, from the very first, the empirical orders with which he will be dealing and within which he will be at home". The latter, "[a]t the other extremity of thought",

> are the scientific theories or the philosophical interpretations which explain why order exists in general, what universal law it obeys, what principle can account for it, and why this particular order has been established and not some other. (Foucault 2002:xxii)

Given the high degree of familiarity that these categories hold, they mostly appear as non-controversial definitions of attitudes, orientation, everyday practices embedded in the law. The smoothness and the apparent simplicity of such identity categories eventuate in a subtle process of naturalization of the features detected by the legislator and fixed in the law. Simplification and the consequent erasure of any problematicity are crucial moves to fulfil what we have seen as one of the main requirements of the law: legal certainty. In the example taken into consideration above, to provide an accountable subject, the legislator has to portray sexuality as an unwavering, unchanging personal characteristic – one that might become a solid reason to justify a crime. To be embedded in the law and to be established as a specific feature to offer protection, sexuality is treated as a feature that arises beyond the legal sphere and exceeds any legal or political fashioning. To consider a subject as worthy of protection, the law addresses her as the bearer of essential feature. She becomes the sexual, sexualized subject of law.

15 A similar point has been made about fn. 4 of the Supreme Court's decision in *United States vs. Carolene Products*, in 1938, in which the "equal protection clause" was debated. Such clause assumed that "courts were particularly obliged to protect minority groups that are chronically vulnerable in the political process" and that "a good way of limiting the [...] judicial interference with political decision making would be to accord special protection only to groups that were 'discrete and insular' – paradigmatically race, national and religious minorities" (Halley 2000:50–51). As in the case of Legge Mancino, lawyers tried to extend such sentence to gender minorities.

16 On sexuality as a choice, see Butler (1989, 1990/1999, 1997d), Butler and Athanasiou (2013), Franklin (1997), Halley (2000), Haraway (1981), Haslanger (2000), Kafer (2013).

The case of sexuality perfectly shows the impact that legal ratification has on identity categories and social perception. Once taken as an essential feature, a natural trait that characterizes a subject in a permanent way, the political value of sexual practices, sexual choices, sexual orientation will decrease dramatically.[17] In fact, as happens with disability, the scale of value to judge and address sexuality can be scientific, medical or even sentimental, but in no way can it involve the recognition of personal agency, responsibility or choice. Sexuality turns into a fate that has to be discovered in humans' genes or in their deep-seated preferences, in their souls (see e.g. Bleier 1984; Fausto-Sterling 1993, 2012; Keller 1995; Spanier 1995). All identity features that undergo processes of legal legitimation incur in this transformation. For the sake of legal certainty, identities cease to be cultural declination of behavioural patterns to turn into natural entities that have to be discovered and posited in the law in their purest form.[18]

Again, sexuality is a typical example to assess the shift that comes about when an attribute or a preference rises to the status of identity. This is particularly tricky when the ratification of an identity category is articulated through a jargon of rights and privileges. In her discussion of the legal impact on the constitution and the delineation of sex and gender, Judith Butler observes that such processes of legal articulation bring about a dangerous double-bind in which sexuality turns into an entity difficult to handle politically (Butler and Athanasiou 2013:35; see also Butler 1990/1999, 1993, 2004a). By building on Leticia Sabsay's work, Butler avers that both the concepts of "choice" and "sexual orientation" are deceptive when used as premises to legal measures. While "choice" can lead to the devaluation of (homo)sexuality as a mere matter of will and arbitrary behaviours[19], the notion of orientation "ascribes a disposition to a subject, and so provides a radically arelational account of sexuality" (Butler and Athanasiou 2013:35). The latter option fosters a conception of sexuality as a natural disposition (indeed, something independent from social relations), occasioning an understanding of sexual orientation as "unchosen". In this sense, "it could qualify [sexual orientation] as an involuntary social characteristic" that "would deserve special protection against discrimination under the law" (Butler and Athanasiou 2013:35). When sexuality is framed in terms of an analogy with either a "political belief" or "disability", the debate on rights takes a binary path which

17 In much the same way, any "personal" choice, when naturalized, loses its *political* value. The political value of personal performances (something that I will address in Chapter 6) invests many areas of people's life. From self-care to the food we eat, personal choices equate to political positionings. In a world mostly driven by corporations and "the Market", in the era of bio-politic, the *personal is now more than ever political.*

18 Political agency concerning sexuality has had a high importance in civil battles. Suffice it to mention the debunking of the idea of maternity as a natural drive for women, or the dismissal of any correlation between hysteria and lesbianism, on these questions, see Cutas and Bortolotti (2010), Braidotti (2003), Cavarero (2014), Denbow (2014), Guaraldo (2015), Haslanger (2006), Kafer (2013), Rich (1986), Wittig (1975). I delve into this issue in Venditti (2014).

19 And so, it would be articulated as a matter of freedom of expression; on this aspect, see Butler (1997b:71 ff), Butler and Athanasiou (2013:33 ff).

hampers the comprehension of such phenomena. On the one hand, the consideration of "sexuality as a kind of right that is borne by a subject [...] appeals to notions of 'free expression' as well as to very culturally specific ideas of what free expression is", to the extent that the "definition that seeks to protect the rights of those who are not free to express their sexuality ends up establishing an ideal, if not a norm, of what the free expression of sexuality should look like" (Butler and Athanasiou 2013:35). On the other hand, ironically, the understanding of sexuality as a natural inclination brings about the same consequence, as a biological account of sexuality would distinguish between a "normal" way of naturally developing one's own sexuality and an "aberrant" one.

This double bind demonstrates that it is the very context in which sexuality has to be relocated that presupposes the affiliation to a structure inadequate to encompass certain phenomena. In being included in the legal field through the production of a category, sexual practices are reduced to a system that simply cannot contain them:

> In this performative intertwinement, gender and sexual categories, identities, and fantasies are reconstituted and reinvented in unforeseen ways as the law "strives" (such a depiction of power as intentional and teleological is only catachrestic here) to produce, affirm, consolidate, thwart, commodify, or render them proper. (Butler and Athanasiou 2013:34)

Generally speaking, we can see how the integration of a specific social practice in the legal body needs to be backed up by a satisfactory "reconstitution" or "reinvention" of the social manifestation of this very practice. If this is the case, then it should come as no surprise that the incorporation of categorized practices into the law cannot but bring forward a crystallization of some aspects of the categories and, consequently, a modification of the social balances they participate in. If some sort of categorization is inevitable in the production of law in general, category-protecting policies go so far as to produce a regulation of social identities based on fixed and reified models.

From this, it follows that the process of categorization opens up distinctive exchanges between the legal body and the social world, and shapes the social and individual perception of identities. If the most blatant consequence is, as I have already shown, the naturalization of certain identities and the smooth process of depoliticization of choices and forms of life, two other questions emerge. These are directly linked with protection and extension of rights, namely the crystallization of identities and the legitimation of specific forms of life.

On the one hand, protected categories undergo a form of crystallization that results from the formalization of categories. While the formalization of any social category produces certain stabilizing effects that see some features being imposed over others and emerge as fundamental, once it is connected with an inclusive purpose, a process of *victimization* is produced. Categories addressed by the law are portrayed as in need of protection and bear as one of their main features the status of "marginalized". Members of these categories are *ipso facto* transformed in the eyes of the law into *victims*.

As observed by Wendy Brown (2000:231), this mode to account for social exclusion relies on a "grammar [that] suggests a condition of constraint [...] foreclosing our hopes in a language that we can neither escape nor wield on our behalf". The crafting and crystallization of a category *as* a vulnerable one implies an immobilization of such designation, which "reinscribes the designation as it protects us". Judith Butler (1997b) articulates this problem in regard to hate speech, casting light on the typical mechanism that structures this type of legal measures. She maintains that the legal ratification of some speech acts *as* hate speech produce, in the very moment in which it sanctions them, the discriminatory act:

> "hate speech" is not deemed hateful or discriminatory until the courts decide that it is. There is no hate speech in the full sense of that term until and unless there is a court that decides that there is. Indeed, the petition to call something hate speech, and to argue that it is also conduct, efficacious in its effects, consequentially and significantly privative of rights and liberties, is not yet to have made the case. The case is made only when it is 'decided.' In this sense, it *is the decision of the state, the sanctioned utterance of the state, which produces the act of hate speech* [...]. Here, the temporal relation in which the utterance of hate speech precedes the utterance of the court is precisely the reverse of the logical relation in which *there is no hate speech prior to the decision of the court.* (Butler 1997b:96, emphasis added)

In much the same way, discrimination against a category *is crafted by the legislator* when a category comes to be delineated and marked as discriminated. This does not mean that – prior to a legal recognition – people do not suffer from marginalization for their sexual conducts or their nonconforming behaviors. But it certainly points at the fact that – prior to a legal *ratification* – a homogeneous "homosexual category" with its standards and well-defined traits does not exist.[20] What I am suggesting here, following Butler, is that some identities are sanctioned in the law as inescapably problematic. Since their access in the legal body redoubles and crystallizes their marginalized position: in being recognized as vulnerable, vulnerability becomes the trademark of these categories, while it is assumed that they will suffer discrimination.

> The paradox, then, is that rights that entail some specification of our suffering, injury, or inequality lock us into the identity defined by our subordination, while rights that eschew this specificity not only sustain the invisibility of our subordination, but potentially even enhance. (Brown 2000:232)

20 On the peculiarity of the Western category of "homosexual", see Fassin (2003) and his studies of the different ways to consider and define *homosexual behaviors* in Eastern Europe and Oriental and African culture. Outside a system of identity rights, homosexual acts *are* considered to be practices that can be performed without retaining a meaning *beyond* the performance itself. People thus might *engage* in homosexual intercourses, but do not take up a *homosexual identity*.

As in the case of the Italian anti-discrimination bill, the law asks subjects to prove their belonging to the identity category it indicates as marginalized. To access the protection issued by the law, subjects must comply with the standards posed in the law. This means that they must accept the identity that ***subjects*** them, in the twofold sense of making them intelligible as subjects of law and of submitting them to the parameters set in the law. To acquire rights, the social actor is called upon embracing a category and displaying a form of compliance.

This form of compliance relies on self-ascription. While laws inspired by category-protecting policies set standards of intelligibility, they do not actively address marginalized subjects.[21] Rather, it supplies a shelter, a special protection *for those who want to make use of it*. This means that the subject herself has the duty to present herself to the law, to ask for protection *on the basis of her being part of a category*.

Here, the third and last question emerges. Category-protecting policies are contingent on the legitimation of specific forms of life, at the expenses of others. This last point arises particularly in the type of recognition engendered by the extension of existing rights to categories that were formerly excluded from benefitting them.

The type of recognition deployed in this case favors inclusion by slightly twisting the form of the existing right. Take, for instance, same-sex marriage: endowing same-sex couples with marital rights does not affect the structure of the institution of marriage. While accessing privileges and seeing their affective relationships legitimized, non-heterosexual couples also enter "a symbolic structure based on ideas of coupledom, monogamy, familial ties, and all those features that traditionally characterize marriage" (Venditti 2019:22). If, at a practical level, this endowment eventuates in a wider participation to legal benefits, at a socio-symbolical level, it replicates the traditional matrix, neglecting the ratification of any possible alternative to an already accepted structure. In other words, the extension of ready-made rights and legal figures to non-traditional forms of life curbs the innovative potential of non-traditional practices. Inclusion, under this form, domesticates and normalizes the emergence of an upsetting practice.

Category-protecting policies not only carve out identity groups and determine their position in the social world, they also support *certain* modes of living at the expenses of others. To give same-sex couples the possibility of accessing marriage or other forms of recognized unions centred on coupledom, monogamy, respectability has its counterpart in the refusal of all the others forms of articulating desires or living affective ties. The legal ratification of same-sex marriage normalizes *an already "normal" desire*, while confirming the inappropriateness of other forms of sexual desire. Paradoxically, the expansion of the categories that can access marriage leaves uncovered (and worsen the marginalization of) those people

21 On the contrary, the right to vote (exemplary of opportunity-oriented policies) is portrayed as a *right* and an *obligation*. In much the same way, the right to education is issued for all people under a certain age. The other types of policies indicate their subject and subject them all.

who are engaged in non-stable, non-monogamous relationships, no matter what their sexual orientation is.

Whether by issuing recognition through protection or through the extension of rights, in the category-protecting approach, inclusion is conceived as deeply linked with the delineation of social categories. The third model of inclusion proceeds from a clear-cut definition of specific strands of the population with a view on promoting tailored measures to tackle marginalization. As the case of the amendment of the Italian law against discrimination makes manifest, categorizing processes carried out at a legal level have to fulfil legal standards of certainty and clarity. In much the same way, to acquire legal recognition, social actors have to exhibit the traits incorporated in the legal body, so as to fall under the clear-cut category presented by the law. The need to retrieve a stable subject of law and the relative requirement for subjects to prove accountable in their belonging to a category create a chain of effects that retain strong sociopolitical consequences. In what follows, I will provide a first analysis of the dynamics engendered by category-protecting policies, to expand on this topic in the next chapters.

The process of categorization, then, opens up distinctive exchanges between the legal body and the social world, and shapes the social and individual perception of identities. From this, three orders of questions emerge. While a more general one concerns the outcomes of a legal fashioning of social categories, other two are directly linked with protection and extension of rights, namely the crystallization of identities and the legitimation of specific forms of life.

It is precisely in this context that a major flaw of the legal inclusion of determinate categories emerges, one that I indicated above as "the constitution of a legitimated stigmatization". As we have seen, the institutionalization of a category happens through the collection and public verbalization of typical traits which mark one's affiliation to a protected category. Those traits become a measure to classify and demarcate social identities, and thus prove crucial to acquire widespread recognition. Nonetheless, as Butler (1997b) and other authors as Wendy Brown (2000) observe, this recognition ends up being "adamantly opposed" to a proper acceptance of problematic identities, in that it "pathologize[s] [...] what ought to be understood instead as one among many human possibilities" (Butler 1997b:76). To put it another way, the institutionalization of identity categories, rather than promoting the acceptance of a plurality of forms of life, eventuates both in a flattening and in a domestication of the nonconforming ones. On one side, it subsumes socially targeted ways of living under the umbrella notion of victims, results in the assimilation of many situations and in the formal erasure of the difference among them. On the other, in forging a univocal model, which implicitly mandates norms of conduct, the institutionalization of identity categories creates unforeseen forms of abjection. For what concerns the threat of victimization, it must be noticed that the protective shelter offered by the law guarantees inclusion, but in such a way that safeguarded subjects come to be permanently marked by the stigma of an unavoidable difference. Legal classifications delineate discriminated categories by operating a separation between those who are considered to be "normal" and those who are bound to be, already and always, outsiders.[22] While the former can autonomously dwell in the social space and confront social threats, the latter is regarded as invariably belonging to a vulnerable group, whose problematic situation hampers the opportunity of a self-sufficient management of one's own social condition. The legal ratification of wretched statuses leads to the active victimization of the marginalized subjects, in that it crystallizes their subaltern position. This form of what can be considered as a legalized oppression is mainly based on the necessary incorporation in the law of those biases that trigger unfairness. This happens because, in order to pursue prejudiced behaviours against vulnerable groups, policymakers have to report and explicitly target those behaviours to the extent that the group itself comes to be constituted in the light of discriminatory traits. The features embedded in the law "reveal the extent to which the basis of the injury [...] is reinscribed in the formulation of rights promising redress" (Brown 2000:235). This marks such kind of policies as deeply paradoxical: rights secure our standing as individuals even as they obscure the treacherous ways in which that standing is achieved and regulated; they must be specific and concrete in order to reveal and redress [...] subordination, yet potentially entrench [...] subordination through that specificity; they promise increased individual sovereignty at the price of intensifying the fiction of sovereign subjects; [...] they move in a transhistorical register while emerging from historically specific conditions; they promise to redress [...] suffering [...] but only by fracturing that suffering [...] into discrete components, a fracturing that further violates lives already violated by the imbrication of racial, class, sexual and gendered power (Brown 2000:238).

The "paradoxical" system enacted by category-protecting policies is grounded precisely in law's appropriation of the injury, so much so that it unwittingly reinforces, or at least reintroduces, the *motives* of discrimination.

On the whole, the analysis of the amendment of the Legge Mancino has revealed the twofold nature of category-protecting policies. The example proposed is particularly interesting, in that it displays the axes along which those policies work: an implicit one, which aims at formally recognizing marginalized categories, and an explicit one, which entails the request for controlling and weakening discriminatory attitudes.[23]

22 It is worth emphasizing that the process of distinction engenders an additional separation, in that the categorization of a definite class leads to highlight only *one* characteristic of the discriminated identity. As Brown (2000:236–237) points out, this strategy fails to give any account of the overlapping of identities.

23 Note that the opponents of the amendment (above all those who belong to a catholic area) harshly criticized the amendment for its potential indirect consequences. In the moment in which homosexual and transgender people are formally recognized by the state, every request for the extension of rights issued by their group would be difficult to dismiss.

4 Millennial rights

A political revolution from the courts

The discussion of the problems that beset category-protecting policies might be integrated with an inquiry into the type of rights on which such policies rely and a comparison between these rights and the kind of rights at play in other policies. Such an analysis should be formal and general at one time. It should investigate the "essence" of rights propounded by category-protecting policies, but at the same time be able to take into account the general setting in which those rights have been produced. Approaching the question of rights and their lexicon in this way allows me to consider a recent but progressive transformation of state law in Western democracies, whose effects have significantly impacted on political discourses and strategies. The aim of such an examination is to offer some insights into the development of a political tool (such as rights) that in the last decades has almost entirely colonized the horizon of political action. In what follows, I intend to elucidate how the grammar of rights is transforming the law and our idea of it, to such an extent that, in the here and the now, the law itself is perceived as innately linked with rights. At present, the connection between rights and law is so strong that the preeminent role of the former within the latter tends to be regarded as the natural and felicitous evolution of democratic legal systems. I will claim that it is a mistake to speak in terms of evolution, if only because the upsurge of rights is quite a recent phenomenon and today's rights look very different from what they did in the past. I will provide the reader with glimpses into the history of rights so as to showcase the different moments that characterize the development of the present legal scenario. My analysis will be both historical and theoretical. I will analyze how the new role of rights has impinged on today's conception of law. Finally, I will discuss the implication of the different rights in use in each of the three policies, with particular attention to the category-protecting one.

The adoption of the grammar of rights, in its current form (see Croce and Salvatore 2015, Grossi 2015; Kennedy 2002, Marzocchi 2004)[1] can be traced back to the first decades of the 20th century, a moment of dramatic uprising that

1 In what follows, I will refer indiscriminately to human and to fundamental rights, since they represent two faces of the same coin, see Marzocchi (2004:19).

led to extensive social transformations. The force of the new model of rights as an instrument to set forth political claims whose strong points are a less disquieting façade and the ability to cross the borders of the juridico-political field. Thanks to this innate manageability, the jargon of rights has the power to reach much broader audiences than erstwhile (more rebellious) forms of political engagement and political claims.

The difficulty of getting to grips with this transformation results in a further miscomprehension of the changes occurred, so much so that the history and evolutionary stages of rights have been read as a coherent trajectory: "[T]he past is treated as if it were simply the future waiting to happen" (Moyn 2010:11). This is, however, a misleading account, since rights have a multifaceted nature and can take different shapes according to the context they are at play. The history of rights cannot be seen as a linear one, as a smooth progression towards their current form.

At present, rights are often analyzed in their connection with democratic processes and state citizenship. Although the nexus among these three elements might appear to be quite plain (as to produce a very neat and clear relationship among them), it is useful to look at it from different angles, in order to account for the different positions that the law – one of the "firmest, deepest and long-held convictions or assumptions of Western political thought" (Marzocchi 2011:12) – takes in relation to other components of the political sphere of Western societies. To do so, I will rely on Virginio Marzocchi's distinction of three legal moments, which makes sense of law's particular position in a given sociopolitical context. The author identifies three levels:

> a a pre-legal and pre-state level, ultimately non-available to humanity, and so able to bind (in normative or anthropological-factual terms) to the next level;
>
> b the level of the law in its being consciously and explicitly established/establishable, that is [the level] of norms [...] which finds in the former [level] (a.) its legitimation together with a criterion of judgement concerning the laws themselves [...];
>
> c the level of power, that is, of the active force which can be employed for the production, administration, enforcement [...] [and] coercive implementation of the law. (Marzocchi 2004:13)

With recourse to this tripartition, it is possible to pinpoint a variety of understandings of law and its relation to politics elaborated on throughout the modern and contemporary eras. The central variable that characterizes these alternative views is the connection between the first and the second level. The first level comprises elements that are claimed to precede the creation and enforcement of laws. Certainly, paradigms that privilege this level might disagree on what these elements are (e.g. the will of God, nature, human beings' natural rights, social normativities; see e.g. Finnis 2011; Kainz 2004), and yet they all agree that these elements are inescapable presuppositions for positive laws to be issued. In this light, the law – whether or not it is understood as the product of human craft – is never entirely fabricated. Pre-eminence accorded to this first level entails that the pre-juridical imposes a limit on the political will of a sovereign (be it an individual or an assembly) and its population. Hence, the production of positive laws has to always take into account what antedates them: the legislative process (which belongs to the second level of this schema) takes as its starting point a set of natural and given tendencies, which have to be considered and integrated in the legal system to establish a just and stable political platform.

The second level represents the legislative activity *par excellence*. In theoretical systems that emphasize this moment, the importance of the first level decreases remarkably. This does not mean that the level of the pre-juridical is completely effaced (for instance, the universality of rights and the importance of social normativities is acknowledged also in some radical-democratic views of law; see e.g. Corradetti 2012); and yet what makes a community a political community is no longer the recognition and ratification of a series of natural, shared traits, but the act itself of issuing laws. Contrary to views that sustain the supremacy of the pre-juridical (where the pre-juridical becomes the foundation of the normative system upon which the political community is premised), views that stress the second level envisage an indelible link between law and politics. From this perspective, law could not be brought about without performing a political action, which in its turn finds its highest, ultimate expression in being legally fashioned.[2]

Keeping this schema in mind, it is possible to gain a privileged point of view on the history of rights and, based on that, to set out to disentangle the multiple trajectories that have led to the crystallization of today's most widespread kind of rights. I already remarked that the last decades, as many authors seem to concur (see Marzocchi 2011, 2014; Moyn 2010), have witnessed a remarkable change in the nature of rights. In between the first and the second half of the 20th century, an unexperienced overturning occurred of the respective roles of the pre-juridical level and the legislative one. This change should not be seen as the mere reshuffling of the levels at play[3] since it ended up reconfiguring not only the role of law and the value of rights, but also the relation between states and citizens.

The first half of the 20th century could be considered as the heir to a modern-democratic conception of the relationship between law and politics, whereby public/political practices are considered as the source of law, which, in its turn, has to make room for actionable instruments for citizens to be able to take part in the political life and to protect themselves, if necessary, against potential threats, either on the part of the state or on the part of their fellow

2 For a full and comprehensive explanation of the relation between these two moments, see Marzocchi (2004:17–21).

3 Marzocchi (2004:24) notes that no process of overturning "represents an authentic innovation, since an upturning change the position of the elements in a relation, leaving both the element and the relation between them substantially untouched".

citizens. The law is the link that ties together single social actors with the public-political sphere. It contributes to the creation of a cohesive community in which people act in accordance with the law because this law is soundly intertwined with the social reality it regulates. In other words, the law presents itself as the manifestation of a political rationality that takes into account the needs and complexities of the reality it governs (Marzocchi 2011:28–29). Even in this scenario, there is a pregiven sphere on which politics is grounded and which in no circumstances can be threatened, defied, unsettled or questioned by the legislator: both politics and law are spheres that have to be integrated with other spheres of society. But how did this conception of the connection among rights, politics and the law come about?

The idea of rights as a juridico-political equipment ideally supplied to all human beings entered the political discourse at end of the 18th century, as the dawning of modern democracies was sealed with the positivization of inalienable natural rights, possessed by every human being.[4] In analyzing the history of rights, Samuel Moyn (2011) contends that modern political thinkers, who understood natural rights as pertaining to each and every subject, paved the way for the incorporation of the jargon of rights into the lexicon of politics. By configuring the single individual as the direct bearer, and the lawful owner, of natural rights that the state was required to respect, these authors favoured the coincidence between the first level and the second level of the law: while rights are impermeable to political power, to be effective, they have to be ingrained in a political order and implemented. On this account, rights are not so much the possession of a human being, as they are ascribed to the *individual as a citizen*. At this point, rights were both *individualized* and *statalized*: rights were indeed a property of individuals, who – in their turn – were conceived as citizens of the state. To draw a parallel with the policies I have examined in the preceding chapters, rights were not attached to a pre-political human being with a specific nature (like in capability-based approach); nor did they address specific categories of citizens requiring protection (as happens in category-protecting policies).

4 I am mainly referring to the *Bill of Rights* adopted in the US from 1776 and to the French *Déclaration des droits de l'Homme et du citoyen*, initially approved in 1789 (see Marzocchi 2004:30–31). In these early documents, fundamental/human rights are still linked to the nation state. They will assume an international configuration only later, when the disasters of World War II called for the introduction of binding international guidelines. The reconstruction I provide in the course of this chapter will not deal critically with the historical definition of "human rights" and with the thorny problem of their ascription. For a reconstruction of what were to be "human" in the former drafts of Bills of Rights, see in general Botti (2012), Cavarero and Restaino (2002), Marzocchi (2004). See also fundamental texts, such as the famous *Déclaration des droits de la femme et de la citoyenne* by Olympe De Gauge (available on-line at https://fr.wikisource.org/wiki/Déclaration_des_droits_de_la_femme_et_de_la_citoyenne, last accessed on 26 October 2018) and Mary Wollstonecraft's (2004) work. An interesting general insight of the exclusionary tendency of human rights is given by the various organizations for human rights, such as the *Worldwide Movement for Human Rights*, https://www.fidh.org/en/ (last accessed on 26 October 2018) and the *Ligue des Droit de l'Homme*, http://www.ldh-france.org (last accessed on 26 October 2018).

Like in opportunity-oriented policies, rights were attached to legal persons that existed insofar as they had a relationship with the state; at the same time, unlike opportunity-oriented policies, they were less of a function of citizenship than the key to approach the political field.[5] Rights guaranteed the fundamental access to the political sphere, because they constituted a virtual link between society and the legislative moment and made sure the law could be affected by those who both belonged to, and participated in, the sociopolitical community. This should be understood as a twofold connection. If, on the one hand, law permeates the social realm thanks to its ongoing relation with law-abiders, on the other hand, citizens took advantage of the law, in that it was the vehicle for actively partaking in the public space. State regulation was designed to open up a cooperative dimension, which was enforced and enforceable as long as citizens themselves were its primary recipients (that is, its primary beneficiaries).

As I alluded to, examples of constitutions that built on such a theoretical background can be found in the various Bills of Rights introduced in the 18th century. These models represent the most vivid instance of the first embodiment of rights into state politics. From that moment onwards, rights became an articulation of the state, to the extent that the former were not thinkable without the latter. Unfortunately, more often than not, these Bills of Rights turned out to be effective only on paper, in that they did not bring about the configuration of public law and private law that they both manifested and presupposed. Rather, they were mainly composed of "philosophical-political statements, which culminated in the enunciation of some liberties thought of in accordance with abstract representations concerning individuals" (Grossi 2015:67; author's translation). In one of his most recent works, Paolo Grossi observes that these Bills of Rights were designed with reference to a philosophical core, and that precisely such a theoretical inclination (which laid emphasis on the need for a recognition of a natural and inherent equality of all humans) resulted in the failure of its own normative intent.[6] In this sense, earlier constitutions set forth lists of rights without specifying what had hitherto been their direct counterpart: obligations.

The elision of this latter moment of commitment and actual enforcement yielded ambiguous results. Even if constitutions were meant to open spaces where citizens could participate in a joint activity of reimagining the state, where rights were taken to serve as creative political tools with a view of fostering the construction of a political community, the model of rights as personal inviolable

5 Opportunity-oriented policies promote rights that give a citizen the possibility of exercising a political function in, as it were, its "administrative" side. Enfranchisement, in this case, takes the form of an admission to some operations, whereas, in its modern configuration, rights were conceived as the proper entrance in the sociopolitical realm. Through rights, the state empowered citizens and gave them the keys for exercising their political agency. On this aspect, see Grossi (2015:36–38; 67–72). Notice that Grossi is very critical of these earlier forms of constitutional rights.

6 A normative intent that, as Grossi (2015) remarks, was designed to govern and regulate society, and exceeded the imposition of a series of precepts from above.

entitlements led to the disavowal of the "relational link of reciprocity" (Marzocchi 2011:26; author's translation) on which the vertical relationship state-citizen, as well as the horizontal relationship among citizens, were based. The creation of a regulation primarily centred on the single individual determined a setback in the sociopolitical arrangement. Rights, affected by the limits so far described, did renegotiate the boundaries of both the political sphere and the authority of the state, but in such a way as to be conducive to a basic opposition between social actors and the state.[7] This passage culminated in the invention of rights as fundamental political instruments that, in advocating the pre-eminence of the pre-juridical, turned modern democracies into a bipolar, poorly integrated system, in which public spaces were no longer the site where social interrelations, civic duties and state norms interacted in a productive way (see Moyn 2014). The new arrangement between the first and the second level gave life to "spaces of citizenship in which rights were accorded and protected" (Moyn 2010:13) as rights, not as routes to democratic production.

Yet, there were still striking differences with what rights would become in the future. While in the modern era, they were by and large marked as pre-juridical entitlements protected by the state, in their contemporary modulation rights acquired the character of supra-state individual liberties as "guarantees of sub-national citizenship [...] restricted to states presumed unreliable in affording the civic entitlement" (Moyn 2010:33). The adoption of a supra-state dimension, however, took place gradually (see Croce and Salvatore 2015:v–xiv, 116–174). More precisely, we can indicate two main landmarks in this evolution. A first one – occurred around 1940 – in which rights "were bound up with international organization" and a second one – occurred around 1990 – in which they were rather linked "with a larger popular language" (Moyn 2010:47). Interestingly, Moyn (see in particular 2014) contends that the former did not lead to what rights are today and harshly criticizes narratives that envisage a link between post-war rights and today's rights. In order to shed light on such a discontinuity, the author focuses on the political value that rights hold in these two epochs, or better, on their position within the political scenario. Although I cannot delve into his historical reconstruction in detail, a little summary of the comparison he draws will be of help.

As I already mentioned, Moyn believes that the basic, essential difference lies in the political role that rights play, and consequently in the place they occupy in the web of sociopolitical connections. Post-war rights still retained a distinctive institutional configuration, whereas "millennial"[8] rights blurred the line

7 For a detailed reflection on the features of "constitutions" and their discrepancies with former Bills of Rights, see in particular Grossi (2005, 2015).

8 The term "Millennials" has come to identify the generation of people born between the 1980s and 2000s in the Global North (Howe and Strauss 2000). At the beginning of the 21st century, this generation took the shape of a cohesive group, whose habits, customs and political stance had the potential to trigger a series of far-reaching changes in the sociopolitical scenario. I apply this formula to the kind of rights that have made their "appearance" around 1990, since, in much

that divides the public, specialized realm of the juridico-political and the private sphere of personal agency and personal entitlements.

Post-war rights were issued on the basis of the idea that the promulgation of an international system of law was necessary for safeguarding and promoting peace. Lawyers and activists involved in peace movements were the main supporters of a legal system that, by creating a cluster of norms enforceable at a domestic level, promoted a basic revision of "the international order to avoid future wars" (Moyn 2010:52). The codification of a set of principles (which only later will be rearguarded as belonging to the level of the pre-juridical) was no symptom of an individualization of rights, as it in no way implied "a turn to the *individual*, let alone *human* rights" (Moyn 2010:182; emphasis added). Therefore, it is clear that supporters of international treatises were not interested in creating a web of norms aimed at shielding the citizens vis-à-vis to the state. Rather they meant to draw up a list of prerogatives and entitlements that might define basic standards of protection for citizens in their countries and maintain peaceful relations among states on account of shared normative assumptions. Nonetheless, the variety of historical and cultural traditions that belonged to the affected parties could not but result in the formulation of a very a-specific set of principles. Eric Posner (2014a, 2014b) observes[9] that, in expressing aspirations of what a human rights "regime" looked like, the Universal Declaration[10] posited a cluster of non-legal instruments, which mirrored the heterogeneous concerns of different blocks.[11] The vagueness that characterized treatises eventuated in the need for institutions that could monitor and interpret the effects of the ratification of the treatises and support the publicization of human rights.

Treatises and charters crafted after 1948 were modelled after modern legislative systems (see Moyn 2012).[12] This resulted in the creation of unsteady normative programmes that, while reflecting the model of national legislations, had their origin in supranational institutions and lacked both powers of enforceability and a direct connection with the people they were addressed to. Treatises seemed to be a first, clumsy attempt to create a post-war international order on the basis of

---

the same period, Western democracies witnessed the rise of a new kind of legal rights that fit the millennial tendency – millennial rights whose dynamics, jargon and political impact were just as unprecedented.

9 See also Moyn (2014), West (2011, 2014), Žižek (2005).

10 Enlarged and emended by other documents aimed at extending rights to more specific segments of society, as, for instance, the *Declaration on the Rights of Disabled Persons* (1975), *Convention on the Rights of the Child* (1989, with two optional protocols adopted in 2000 and 2002), *Universal Declaration on Cultural Diversity* (2001) and so on. On this, see Marzocchi (2004, 2015), Moyn (2012).

11 Posner (2014) identifies two (plus one) main blocks: the US, which was interested in a liberal inflection of human rights and pursued the direction of individually-inflected political rights; and the Soviet Union, that pushed for a socioeconomic articulation of human rights. Finally, European states stood in the middle, alternatively expressing their interest in both strategies.

12 Moyn (2010:183–185) reports the effort of many scholars and lawyers in framing human rights in continuity with modern legal thinking and in accordance with "the most traditional foundations of state sovereignty".

the reproduction of nation-state dynamics and in a scenario in which the state authority was still perceived as supreme. Therefore, ambivalence becomes the mark of such post-1948 Declarations,[13] for three reasons. First, they embodied "the temptation to blame twentieth-century disaster on the 'positivism' according to which all valid norms originated in the state", but still neglected the appeal to natural laws as "a viable alternative". Second, the "same ambivalence surrounded the turn to the individual as a potential subject of international law" (Moyn 2010:182), because the system of rules was intended to maintain an intra- and supra-state balance among states but addressed individual citizens. Third, the creation of international charters of rights was achieved "at the price of legal enforceability" (Moyn 2010:186), in that no system of enforcement was put in place. In this scenario, human rights took the form of a quixotic experiment designed to avoid threats to international peace and security,[14] without engaging in a sound reformation of the international system in which they could and should be implemented. The alleged natural origin of human rights, which was the linchpin of these documents, neglected the cultural background from which they came, and at the same time, generally overlooked their social and economic side (Holmes and Sunstein 1999; Posner 2014a). The scant engagement with a more tangible dimension of human rights can be easily explained when we look at the theoretical and practical difficulties inherent in the "proposal of some to make individuals direct subjects of international law and to grant them a right of action in a special international court against their own state" (Kunz in Moyn 2010:189).[15] States should commit themselves to a project that severely limited their authority,[16] by increasing both the power of a supranational assembly and the power of individuals, who, in appealing to a supranational authority, were no longer to be considered as mere state citizens.[17] The thorny issue of sovereignty that arose from this situation ended up being at the basis of the establishment of specific supranational courts. This is what marks another passage of the transformation I am describing here. In fact, if in the 18th century, fundamental rights were still heavily dependent on the mediation of the legislator (and thus underwent a moment of national interpretive formulation), 20th-century rights took the form of superimposed guidelines that compelled the national legislative

13 On the ambiguity of human rights, see also Archibugi and Bentham (1998).

14 See Marzocchi (2004:48).

15 Both Moyn (2010:190–194; see also 2012) and Marzocchi (2004:67) observe that even in addressing single individuals, human rights are affected by ambiguities. It was in fact unclear who had to be considered the addressee of rights (the citizen? the individual? the individual as member of a population?). Such a problem emerged particularly when the post-colonial discourse appeared in the public forum: self-determination came up as a collective right, but nonetheless the collectivization of such a right was exposed to many flaws.

16 See Moyn (2014), West (2014), Grossi (2015).

17 Marzocchi (2004:62–70) and Posner (2014) underline the effort of those states that decided to include in their legislations the principles formulated by the Assembly. When included in national legislations, human rights turn into privileges ascribed to citizens, and then lose their universal predisposition.

rationality instead of permeating it and strengthened single social actors instead of fostering the cohesion of the political community.

The following sections will provide an account of the outcomes of the opposition produced by 20th-century rights between popular sovereignty and state legislative self-determination (Marzocchi 2004:37). To do so, I will examine the effects of the different kinds of rights I have addressed so far in and on the contemporary scenario.

Before proceeding, though, let me stress again that millennial rights should not be considered as the static endpoint of a long journey that began at the end of the 18th century. Although they retain the same basic features that characterized 1948's rights formula, the very last decades set an important threshold for human/fundamental rights, to the extent that today's rights can be said to hold a very tenuous connection with the ones of the 18th century. It should be recognized that they constitute a specific moment in the history of rights and perform a distinctive role in the stabilization and renegotiation of international sociopolitical and financial balances. Millennial rights are the latest formulation of fundamental/human rights, but, most probably, will not be the last, let alone the ultimate. The chain of transformations that have led to the ratification of treatises and to the creation of courts is still in motion. Although the future of rights is hardly predictable, a careful and in-depth comprehension of the transformations that occurred in the 20th century, and more notably in its last decades, is key to grasping the sociopolitical force of rights. My suggestion is that the core of their pre-eminence and influence largely depends on two (deeply connected) processes: a theoretical one (alien to the first wave of rights), namely *essentialization*; and a historical one, that, with Duncan Kennedy (2001), I call "*popularization*". The explanation of such processes will make sense of the current fortune of rights and their jargon.

Essentialization and popularization are hardly distinguishable. However, for analytical purposes, I will examine them separately, starting with the former because of its multifaceted and composite character. Generally speaking, essentialization is the process through which contingent (cultural and historical) assumptions turn into *naturalized* entities, so much so that they appear as *universally* valid. If various notions of essence, nature and universality are very often entrenched, the case of rights makes no exception. The rhetoric at play conceives human/fundamental rights as something that originates in a pre-political, pre-cultural and ahistorical realm, that is, as something that is established in/by nature and pertains to the humankind as a whole. Again, Marzocchi's tripartition is useful to clarify further what essentialization is. However, it will be necessary to make some adjustments with the purpose of grasping the peculiarity of millennial rights.

Drawing from Marzocchi's discussion (2004:13–14), we can observe that in the political arrangement hallmarked by the rising of millennial rights, essentialization takes the form of an expansion of the pre-juridical level, which gains pre-eminence over the others. The origin of human/fundamental rights fall within the scope of the pre-juridical, which is not (and has not to be) "adulterated" by culture-specific or contextual elements. Hence, rights are credited with the natural quality of universality, with the result that existing political communities' legal consciousness is informed by an idea of rights as ahistorical entities, embedded in humans' own genetic makeup. Once they get to be seen as fundamental and human, rights affirm themselves as an essential and extra-temporal aspect of a legal system that has to constrain positive law and in no way can be questioned or even revised by any political (that is, public and deliberate) decisions.

From this point of view, the supremacy of the pre-juridical must be considered as the engine of a transformation of the law-making system. The elevation of "natural" human features to the status of rights elides (or at least conceals) the reflexive process that underpins the production of laws, and thus flattens the legislative level. Rights (whether natural or positive) appear, and impose themselves, as pregiven entities that the legislator is called upon to recognize and make explicit. Millennial rights subordinate legislative choices, to the extent that not only can the legislator count on a restricted authority, but in addition, this very authority is conditional upon the legislator's capacity to bring out and support pregiven natural assumptions with binding force. This ends up weakening the level of legal enforceability, since the status of obligation and its position in relation to entitlements change. Obligations are no longer the product of a political decision – which is valid inasmuch as it is justifiable and actually justified through deliberative processes. Rather, obligations are the positive expression of a negative political posture. Moreover, most of the obligations come to be imposed on the state, placing no burdens on citizens. Rights, as we have seen, are couched in the form of entitlements and privileges for single individuals, while they represent the limit beyond which there can be no state injunctions. They are the sphere, the field, which the state has to safeguard, while having no power to control it.

This reading aptly displays the effects of the increasing influence of the pre-juridical in a political system based on rights. Nonetheless, my suggestion is to use Marzocchi's scheme to analyze essentialization as a process that takes place at each of these three levels. In this perspective, I see essentialization as a *model* that underlies the expansion of rights but can change its shape according to the level it emphasizes. Essentialization takes respectively three forms, namely, *naturalization*, *political universalization* and *identitarian essentialization*.

Stress on the pre-juridical level eventuates in a *naturalization* that underscores the *human* aspect of millennial rights. This is what happens in capability-based policies. Instead, when the legislative level is emphasized, rights are formulated as *fundamental*. Here, rights are no longer linked to a natural condition, but to a *political* one, seen as fundamental for the enjoyment of citizenship (whether national or global). This is what happens in opportunity-oriented policies. Finally, the supremacy of the moment of enforceability leads to the institution of *identitarian* rights, which grant entitlements in accordance to some personal features. This is what happens in category-protecting policies. For, the connection between the third level and the recognition of certain rights to specific categories has to be found in the condition of their implementation. Identitarian rights are instruments supplied to private social actors (whether single individuals or groups), who can bring their cases to courts in order to promote their causes and to pursue institutional recognition.[18] Enforceability is no longer the task of a determinate political body, but becomes the domain of the judicial, which, with its legitimate power to issue coercive judgments, assumes something that comes close to an executive role. In other words, the adjudicative moment takes over the executive, which, in its turn, is assimilated by the conjoint action of single initiatives and courts' judgements. Each of these modulations (all conducive to some sort of essentialization) highlights some characteristics of millennial rights over others. Let me explore them in more detail.

The naturalization of rights is conditional upon their anchorage to supra-cultural factors, which are claimed to appertain to human nature. As emerged from the examination of capability-based strategies and the examples discussed in that context, the tendency to structure policies along the idea that political institutions have to safeguard the kernel of human capacities takes a very definite path when based on the rhetoric of rights. Naturalization represents a key element in the affirmation (both historical and ideological) of human rights. A view of naturalization[19] as a process through which liberal capitalist democracies have structured rights, disclosing the Western ideological imaginary, that is, reflecting the historical legacy of European and, broadly speaking, the Global North is supported by Slavoj Žižek (2005). In Žižek's elaboration, we can identify three main directions along which the naturalization of rights (or, in other words, the re-naturalization of traits culturally ascribed to human beings) has taken place. Millennial rights modelled on a scheme that privileges the pole of the pre-juridical have often been formulated as, first, the right to choose freely, second, the right to self-determination and, third, the right to individual protection. In spite of their being disguised as necessary features for the development of every human being (to the extent that they have come to represent the core of humanity), such rights bespeak the need to reinforce a governmental model that is deeply intertwined with history of the West and its culture. The re-instantiation of these rights in nature turns the relative political entitlements (usually considered as the outcome of a public-discursive procedure) into something that appertains to the single human subject *per se*.

Žižek's understanding of human rights fits perfectly the analysis of the flaws of capability-based policies. By taking on a more general perspective, the author demonstrates that essentialization, and as a consequence, the creation of a reified notion of the "human being" produces two effects: on the one hand, it provides an account of differences as capricious attitudes of single individuals; on the other, it impoverishes the value and weight of political institutions. Broadly

18 For an account of these dynamics, see, in particular, Goldoni (2014), Marzocchi (2014), Menski (2014).

19 Although Žižek (2005) calls this process "essentialization", his account reflects my formulation of naturalization; accordingly, I will refer to his theory but avoid faithful reference to terms he uses.

speaking, human rights lead to an indefinite deferral of the moment of variance – so as to hamper the very ***articulation*** of differences – and, at the same time, count on the creation of a series of non-political bodies meant to embed this space of humanity that cannot be administered politically. These two conditions underlie the "triple specification" of human rights that Žižek elaborates on.

Freedom of choice and self-determination imply the displacement of individual preferences out of the political realm. The right to choose freely is counterpointed by the impossibility of making a choice that does not reflect the kind of humanity modelled on the typical, value-laden and culture-specific subject of the West.[20] Therefore, the naturalization of an alleged freedom of choice bars the expression of an individuality that does not embody the hegemonic paradigm indicating what a human being is to be. In this scenario, diversity is tolerated insofar as it does not appear as disruptively conflicting or insofar as it can be understood as one's idiosyncratic caprice and not as a more general practice posing a threat on mainstream ones. When practices that fall outside the scope of this notion of humanity are enacted in a non-individual and non-idiosyncratic way, but as alternative and deliberate patterns of action, they bring about tensions and are perceived as potential menaces.[21] In much the same way, individuals are required to adhere to a forceful pursuit of self-determination, as to a "politics of *jouissance*", which is generally reduced to the task of achieving a (compelling) gratification and satisfaction. The impossibility of not embracing the fulfilment of one's own affirmation, that is, the derogation to the "right to pleasure", follows from the same assumptions that structure the idea of choice as the proclamation of an individual, a-relational liberty.[22] Under this guise, humanity is nothing but an abstract condition of willingness – one that cannot be woven in a web of concrete orders and systems, since every single nuance or habit constitutes a potential infringement of the pure human condition. At a substantial level "[w]hat I am, in terms of my concrete social or cultural background, is experienced as contingent, since what ultimately defines me is the 'abstract'

20 This question has been famously addressed by Gayatry Chakravorty Spivak (1988), when she describes the bounded situation of the widow's self-immolation in the pyre (she is unspeakable both in the eyes of the colonizers – if she decides to sacrifice herself – and in the eyes of the indigenous – if she decides not to follow the tradition). See also Žižek's work (2005:2–4) where he bring up the question of the *hijab*.

21 Žižek (2005:6) refers to "pacifist militarism" as an example of this contradictory tendency. Differences are "tolerated" as long as they do not prove disruptive of the established system and the preservation of it must be pursued by all means. Thus war becomes "acceptable insofar as it seeks to bring about peace, or democracy, or the conditions for distributing humanitarian aid".

22 With "a-relational" I refer to a kind of radical a-relationality that not only separates the single agent from other agents and its community, but results in a sort of idiosyncratic estrangement. Liberty, choice, self-determination, when described as individual *rights* (to which we are entitled), become the expression of a univocal willing, that cannot but impose its own presence in an authoritarian, narcissistic, acritical way. The world outside and its components are just accidental happenings on the path of such a willing. For an idea of the disposability of the others (whether human, animal, water or Mother Earth), see Braidotti (2013), Butler (2000, 2004a, 2005), Neimanis (2009, 2014).

universal capacity" that makes me a human being. "Likewise", Žižek (2005:14; emphasis added) observes,

> any object that can satisfy my desire is experienced as contingent, since my desire is conceived as an 'abstract' formal capacity, indifferent to the multitude of particular objects that may, but never fully do, satisfy it. [...] *I experience myself as an individual who is not directly 'born into' his social role.*

In much the same way as happens in the disjointed regulation concerning the everyday life of people with disability, human rights tend to displace personal affections of single individuals' lives. Traditions, cultural background as well as nonconforming desires, preferences and traits are treated as non-diriment. Not only does such a denial pave the way for the annihilation of a public and political management of society (of which I will speak in a few pages), it also supports the legitimation of a hegemonic position while covering it under the diaphanous veil of a bogus universalistic ideology. Basically, it denies the cultural impulse at the origin of human rights, neglecting that pre-juridical entities are nothing but the expression of a series of political practices. It belies "political process that sustains all these non-prepolitical relationships" and conceals that in "human society, the political is the encompassing structuring principle, so that every neutralization of some partial content as 'non-political' is a political gesture par excellence" (Žižek 2005:11).

Finally, today's conformation sanctifies individual protection. In order to safeguard the single individual, the law takes the shape of a set of instruments that are not primarily arranged for creating a context of common political interaction, since they mainly aim at delineating a space in which social actors can freely exercise their rights. Individual protection (the last point of Žižek's triangle) entails the contraction of the state's commissions and consequently, the extension of individual's competences and the expansion of non-political ways of administering the social field.

In Žižek's terms the retrenchment of the state generates an "obscene double-supplement of power", in which the dimension of a public exercise of power (that characterizes Western's political democracies) makes room to the headless wielding of private powers. What he finds "obscene" in such a diffraction of power is its intrinsic connection with violence (see e.g. Butler 1997a, 1997c, 1997d; Butler and Spivak 2007). Since it affects political power from "outside" and supports it by providing a surplus of meaning, this violence is not *strictu senso* political (see also Bourdieu 1991; Butler 1997b, 1997c; Moati 2014). As has been already noticed, power and authority tend to be coupled with the rhetoric of a natural origin, a pre-juridical and pre-political derivation that substantiates them through the provision of an ultimate justification.[23] Therefore, violence

23 An example of the circularity of this sort of reasoning can be found in Butler's (1990/1999, 1993) famous assumption that sex does not "cause" the ascription to a determinate gender, but rather that is the cultural articulation of gender that allows us to recognize two different sexes; see also Felman (2002), Wittig (1975).

takes the shape of a political gesture unfolded in the act of founding authority in a pre-juridical and alleged natural space (see also Bourdieu 2004). Thus, the double supplement of power is tantamount to the imposition of a cultural, political and contingent set of assumptions mediated by an essentialization. From this point of view, the delegation of political power entails the weakening of a public authority (which is both questionable and testable),[24] in favour of a multiplicity of instances which often happen to be non-political organizations in control of different segments of the social field.

When emphasis is placed on the legislative level, naturalization gives way to another form of essentialization. Rights organized on the basis of legal/political traits are no longer centred on the extension of entitlements on the basis of humanity. Linked to political affiliation, such rights aim at safeguarding basic entitlements for those who are part of a political community. This is the reason why I decided to use the label "fundamental" to define those rights. Millennial rights that stress the legislative moment are not related to national citizenship in itself, but rather are conferred on multiple levels on a political basis.[25] Opportunity-oriented strategies, which develop policies aimed at granting basic political rights, constitute an instance of this kind of rights as occurring at different political levels. These rights are grounded on four central features: the political community they aim to affect; the subjects they address; the claims they put forward; and the goals they pursue.

Like human rights, fundamental rights pursue the aim of providing entitlements for the largest number of people, so that the notion of political affiliation proves to be a distinguishing trait only in the face of the fact that political communities are nowadays very different from modern ones. Namely, fundamental rights reach out to a political formation that has (potentially) no boundaries. Unlike the nation-state, which is necessarily limited in space and time, fundamental rights might extend to a boundless political space. On account of that, they are often portrayed as exportable and able to encompass an ever-increasing number of social actors. The possibility of an indefinite growth entails the transformation of the legislative tool, as well as the transformation of the tasks and traits of the legislator. Providing norms for a diffracted and multilayered political community means eschewing the role of governing in its purest and strongest

24 Let me once again point out that the same structure of "human rights" triggers the transferral of authority from the state to private bodies; see Marzocchi (2004).

25 Kate Nash (2009:1072) analyzes the complex question of citizenship in a post-national political horizon, introducing the notion of "'actually existing' cosmopolitan citizenship". In her words: "'Actually existing' cosmopolitan citizenship is characterized by a proliferation of status groups. The members of each group enjoy a different package of formal and substantive rights according to their situation as citizens or non-citizens, the way in which states administer human rights, and their access to material and moral resources within that state". Nash distinguishes between "actually existing" citizens in "super-citizens", "marginal-citizens" (Nash 2009:1073), "quasi-citizens" (Nash 2009:1076), "sub-citizens" and "un-citizens" (Nash 2009:1078), showing the interrelations and overlaps among different legislations to which these "existing citizens" are (or are not) subjected.

sense (Grossi 2015) – that is, as a form of planning and organizing, managing and regulating a community in view of its shared projects.

In order to extend basic political entitlements to a non-national community, fundamental rights must be attachable to minimal political units that inhabit the political space but are not defined in accordance to this belonging. In this sense, the "citizen", the abstract subject that opportunity-oriented rights address, is replaced by another abstract and general entity: the individual social actor. It is in the identification of these individual social actors as bearers of fundamental rights that essentialization occurs again. Although the subject of fundamental rights is a political one, in the increasing fluidification of the political community, she is the only anchor to her political identity. Political universalization presupposes the essentialization of the "citizen", who becomes an *alter-ego* of the human being: such a political subject is universal and does not depend on any political structure. In fact, the citizen only transits in these structures, precisely by exercising her rights and entitlements. As such, the political subject has no background: she is universal and universalized, enfranchised and right-holder, but in no way can she be part of a more complex web of sociopolitical relations. In other terms, the lack of background results in a double lack of social terrain and interpersonal context.[26] In this scenario, fundamental rights reinforce the status quo of a citizen that may hold sway over her political status,[27] but that is hardly considered in her concrete existence. This is why fundamental rights can be said to be epitomized by opportunity-oriented policies. Here, rights and policies take into account an abstract subject whose universality and radical autonomy are detrimental both to the political community and to single individuals.

Fundamental rights end up *being at the same time pre-juridical entities and the expression of a political virtue.* They glue together the force of the normative argument and the force of legislative authority. It is in such a combination between an inborn connection with the legal sphere and a recognized existence outside the legal system that Duncan Kennedy (2002) locates the key factor behind the success of rights talk in the contemporary political scenario. The bifid nature of fundamental rights turns them into a device that actualizes a mediation "between the domain of pure value judgments and the domain of factual judgements" (Kennedy 2002:184). Given that, any appeal to rights (whether issued in courts or in parliaments) mobilizes at one and the same time a normative judgement and a proposal for a concrete resolution. The twofold composition of rights offers a platform that, in being universal and broadly accessible (since not

26 Many commentators have found in Aeschylus's Antigone a good allegory for developing a reflection about the transcendence of the "citizen" and the consequent detachment of this figure from a broader, lively cluster of social – and psychic – interrelation. In this respect, I find particularly illuminating Butler's (2000) and Cavarero's (1997:13–26) readings of Antigone's role as a disturbing, disruptive voice in an androcentric, fallogocentric political horizon.

27 See the *International Covenant on Civil and Political Rights*, in particular Part I, Art. 1; available online at http://www.ohchr.org/en/professionalinterest/pages/ccpr.aspx (last accessed on 26 October 2018).

only experts have acquaintance with it), also provides the basis for an "objective, rational, determinate discussion of how [rights] ought to be instantiated in social or legal rules" (Kennedy 2002:185). Millennial rights prove to be, as Kennedy has it, "factoid", that is, suitable for providing clear instructions on how to implement the values they convey. Kennedy observes that the "general project of social rationality" that emerges out of fundamental rights cannot but rest on "interpretive fidelity rather than [on] mere legislative preferences" (Kennedy 2002:185). In saying so, he accentuates the specific essence of rights, which have first and foremost to be transposed into the legal system rather than be crafted by the legislator.

It comes as no surprise that fundamental rights pursue a goal that we have seen to be considered by many scholars (and to find a large consensus among laypeople) the acme of democracy[28]: equality. The demand for equality is one of the typical marks of millennial rights, since they entail a call for "equality in a special sense" (Kennedy 2002:182). Rights, between the last decades of 20th century and the beginning of the new millennium, "did not involve the demand for equality in the distribution of income or wealth between social classes, regions, or communities, but rather [ask for] 'equal protection' for individual members of previously subordinated social groups" (Kennedy 2002:182). In this new configuration, equality stood for the ratification of a plethora of discriminated groups and individuals, who had to be politically sustained in their right to be treated equally. The universal goal of equality was by then formulated in terms of a right, which led to a gap between national legislation and the basic right of equality. A demand for equality, when presented under the form of a universal right of the individual (or better, of the citizen) bears pragmatic effects on the legal discourse and on the legal arrangement. First, it is possible to frame claims and demands by using the jargon of rights, with the consequence that any social actor can potentially resort to the language of the fundamental right to equality for substantiating pleas for change or for calling for amendments of national legal systems. This strategic use of such a fundamental right deeply modifies its essence: it is no longer a guideline or a principle. It becomes a "positive prescription" (Kennedy 2002:195) to be interpreted and incorporated in the national legal system. By the same token, the bifid nature of fundamental rights renders them both part of a political reasoning and the expression of a universal drive, with the result that, for instance, the right to equality is considered to be an "open-textured [argument derived] from morality, social welfare, expectations, and institutional competence and administrability" (Kennedy 2002:196). Such a combination of pre-juridical and juridical traits favours the *popularization* of legal reasoning, which ceases to be the property of legal experts and enters the political, social and personal discourse at many levels. In this sense, the rights talk is the carrier of two intermingled existences: a legal, institutional one, and

28 On this, see generally, Duggan (2003), Gilden (2008), hooks (1994), Lacey (1997, 1998), Lonzi (2010).

a "lay", social, naturalized one. If Kennedy's reading, on one side, confirms the main degenerative processes that are occurring at the legal level (the lack of reflexivity and the legitimation of the legislator), on the other, it makes visible further implications that arise in the creation of fundamental rights.

Fundamental rights come to be placed in the sphere of non-negotiability, where "rights are just legal rules, more or less abstract, more or less easy to administer", but with something more, which divides them from "other legal materials" (Kennedy 2002:197). In their strictly positive usage, rights become instruments in the hands of social actors, and yet they are loaded with a symbolic weight, which becomes invisible precisely because in their legal usage (in their being both "rules and reasons for rules" [Kennedy 2002:182]) the reflexive moment of political elaboration gets lost. Fundamental rights empower the individual at the cost of shattering the social fabric and the political rationality of the public discourse. The legislature loses its authority (it encompasses but does not produce norms) and its reflexive stance. What is more, fundamental rights generate a language which becomes suitable for translating semantic contents from one medium to another. Rights talk is premised on the universalization of partial and contingent presuppositions, which are re-instantiated in the social sphere through the appealing to this language. The force of this translation is nicely captured by Kennedy (2001:214):

> When people want to claim things from the legal system, they put their demands into rights language, as they once put them in religious language. But rights are more than just a language – or we might say that, like any language, rights talk does more and less than translate a clear and constant meaning from one medium to another. Rights talk was the language of the group – the white male bourgeoisie – that cracked open and reconstituted the feudal and then mercantilist orders of Western Europe, and did it in the name of Reason. The mediating power of the language, based on the presupposition of fact/value and law/politics distinctions and on the universal and factoid character of rights, was a part of the armory of this group, along with the street barricade, the newspaper, and the new model family.

The inquiry into the three types of essentialization ends up with the examination of what I have called "identitarian rights". These rights do not emphasize either the human being's pre-juridical, natural essence or the subject's political stance; instead, they insist on the centrality of some personal features. Here, essentialization concerns single aspects of people's identities with the result that scattered and disjointed attachments of one's individuality are turned into representative characteristics of the subject vested with rights. In this way, rights are no longer configured as human or fundamental, but as identitarian, as they are attached to specific identity elements that come to be treated as providing a comprehensive description/definition of those who exhibit them. Essentialized features provide a totalizing representation of the subject, as they capture the subject of rights through a universally recognizable and actually recognized description of a naturalized and stable identity.[29] What is more, essentialized features become the grounds for the conferral of rights. It should be noted, though, that in the case of identitarian rights, such ratified traits are not elements that delineate human beings regardless of their active participation, for these characteristics can be possessed (or lacked), and thus can grant (or prevent) access to identitarian rights, only if subjects recognize themselves as possessing them. This is the reason why the kind of essentialization at play in identitarian rights is strongly connected with the implementation of rules. While human and fundamental rights become compelling at the very moment in which they are issued (since the subject is entitled to such rights for the bare fact that she is a human being or a member of a political community), identitarian rights, in order to be activated, have to be claimed by the subject. Therefore, if millennial rights in general have a special relation to enforceability,[30] identitarian ones hasten the transformative process of the administrative moment. Identitarian rights mark a shift in the nature of rights: from a cluster of guidelines that, to be enforced, have to be encompassed by political institutions, they become a set of entitlements directly available to citizens. In most cases (differences depending on the structure and the tradition of national legal systems), identitarian rights exist as principles issued by courts, and the trigger of the judicial action is *the single individual's* claim to these rights. To such an extent, rights exist in a space that is not only supranational, but that is also ultra-juridical: as a truly specific and quite recent legal tool (offered and accessible to laypeople), identitarian rights exit the legal space and get entrenched in common, everyday parlance. In such a circular intercourse – which I will explore in detail in Chapter 5 – people recognize themselves in legally codified identities and understand themselves in accordance with the image produced by courts. Identitarian rights turn out to be something more than a manageable instrument to perform political effects. Oppressed groups and discriminated people are invested with a new and unprecedented sociopolitical power, one with which they can assume a sharper political position and achieve social visibility. When identitarian rights enter the scene, marginalized people can benefit from such a bifid tool, which can be used both to gain access to basic rights and to describe one's own position in the social

29 This statement might sound slightly obscure, but I will delve into it in due course. For now, it suffices to say that – as happens with the introduction of category-based policies – single traits of the subject take over her entire personal representation. In this sense, they are naturalized, because identities turn into indelible and totalizing marks. Moreover, those marks are universalized, because they are suitable for describing *all* the subjects who embrace the ratified identity.

30 Enforceability is no longer a central feature in all those policies that take on the rhetoric of rights, since, as Marzocchi (2004:24–27) notices, the latter inverts the hierarchy between obligation and entitlement, state and citizen. Moreover, the creation of supranational courts and legislative organs has a huge impact on enforceability since nation states are called upon respecting supranational rules (Croce and Salvatore 2015; Goldoni 2014; Marzocchi 2004, 2014; Menski 2014), but at the same time there is no supranational organ to control how (if and when) such rules are implemented (Posner 2014).

world. In sum, identitarian rights are something more than a political weapon: they are narrative tools with performative effects.[31]

With the rise of identitarian rights,[32] the jargon of rights acquires a twofold existence. At a legal level, it is the vehicle of a political device for laying claims, constitutively rooted in the concept of identity. In this sense, it constitutes a flexible instrument for articulating interests and demands, while structuring the conflict in a "positive" way (in opposition with the "oppositive" way of the political struggles of the '60s and the '70s, see Merry 2006). This gives laypeople the possibility of framing their political claims in a less "problematic" way, as well as the opportunity to have recourse to an impartial judge to have their claims redeemed. At a personal level, the jargon of rights functions as a paradigm, a model allowing people to gain social visibility. Essentialization turns personal traits into natural and stable elements through which people can describe a shared condition, which then becomes recognized as "real". Basically, the jargon of rights furnishes a novel grid of intelligibility, a means for being seen and heard, for being recognized in society, in virtue of a higher-level recognition.

I would like to conclude this chapter with a brief overview of the outcomes of the success of millennial rights. While the discussion exposed above helps understand mechanisms engendered singularly by particular types of rights, an overall account is useful to showcase the political weight they exert at present.

Those who criticize the "millennial twist" of rights define them as "positively harmful to the party of humanity" (West 2011:714). This conclusion is based on the idea that, as Robin West (2011:718–719; see also West 2014) remarks, 20th- and 21st-century rights are not only likely to weaken the democratic process and complicate the fulfilment of equality projects.[33] Ultimately, they also prove to be detrimental to vulnerable subjects as they give life to an uneven social realm,[34] characterized by a radical fragmentation (or even a fractalization – see also Grossi 2015; Marzocchi 2004, 2014) of the political community and by the insulation of the private sphere, which remains (or better, *has* to remain) untouched (so, in the end, unheard and unseen) by state policies.

31 On the value of the terms we have access to in order to speak and provide a narration of ourselves, see Butler (2005).

32 Kennedy (2002:181–183) speaks of a passage from "class politics" to "identity politics" that took place in the 60s. The uprisings of this period that were hallmarked by widespread violence, in which claims were put forward in quite a violent way (usually under the form of struggles and political recrimination), led to a milder form of manifestation, in which groups' demands were articulated as pleas and addressed to courts in order to be recognized. This less problematic way of claiming for recognition proved to be more effective in the long run and paved the way for the contemporary management of sociopolitical clashes.

33 Respectively, as I have largely explained, by hampering the legislative process and formulating a notion of equality that heavily relies on unfair premises.

34 West (2011), among others (see, for example, Brown and Halley 2002), maintains that the degeneration of rights – which were conceived as a vehicle for the liberation of oppressed groups and as a guarantee of peace and solidarity – depends on both their structure (that we can describe as, at least, individualistic) and the fact that they are integrated in a liberal-conservative system, which increases and fosters some of the ambiguous dynamics engendered by millennial rights.

It is of help to recall Grossi's (2015) observation that the very system of millennial rights sparks and increases such degenerative processes. This is because the morphing of single individuals into the sole subjects of rights and the empowerment of private social actors – favoured by supranational authorities and ratified by national ones – causes an overlap among different and coextensive authorities. In this scenario, while it is up to judicial authorities to secure the application of rights (mainly conceived by international bodies) and it is up to the private individual to activate the appropriate legal tools, national political institutions withdraw from their traditional place and delegate their tasks – without formally relinquishing their supreme powers. It would be naive to consider such a tightening of the state only as a "damage" caused to the state by the explosion of private and/or supranational entities. Rather, the retraction of national political institutions is the symptom of an "incompetence" of "a sub-minimal or failed state" (West 2011:731). When the rhetoric of human/fundamental rights invades the political space of such "failed states", it serves as an alibi for, and an easy solution to, their decay. Nation states are finally relieved from the burdensome function of safeguarding civil society and the public sphere as well as that of promoting order, because they tend more and more to rely on pre-ordered solutions that they are required to recognize and ratify. In this sense, it is possible to look back at the implementation of imposed guidelines as the aware decision of the national sovereign authority to limit itself, so as to drop some of its basic functions (Grossi 2015). To put it roughly, by exercising its authority and by formally heeding the call of rights, the state eschews its duties and subtracts from its own jurisdiction some spheres and areas of people's everyday lives.[35] However, such a withdrawal has its effects on the citizens, who – in finding themselves deprived of a series of politically organized supporting nets – invoke the right to "exit [...] from the social compact" governed by an organization that fails "to perform basic, fundamental [...] functions" (West 2011:730). In this context, the public sphere runs the risk of being dismantled (Marzocchi 2004:41–42), as the institution itself of millennial rights accelerates both its "segmentation" and its "decomposition". West is adamant that, if placed in such a structure, only rhetorically do rights promote the revitalization of a wealthy, healthy and fair sociopolitical fabric, while actually fostering subordination, alienation and generally curb social mobility.

However, it is precisely in the deployment of rights' rhetorical resources that the regime of rights has conclusively been established. The language that underlies rights (completely oriented towards the individual) provides (experts *as well as*

35 The recognition of imposed rights and the limitation of the state's own authority can be easily justified by embracing the perspective of a national state that is increasingly shrinking. From this point of view, the adoption of supra-national instances follows a political strategy of survival. This can be either economic, where the implementation of rights is contingent on the enjoyment of economic benefits (see e.g. Goldoni 2014; Posner 2014) or strictly political, where the state relies on international interventions for the management of everyday incumbencies (see West 2011).

lay people; see Kennedy 2002:180) a flexible vehicle for formulating interests and claims. The rights talk constitutes a new constellation of sociopolitical meanings. The vocabulary developed in the issuing of rights has expanded and popularized by the growing reliance of single individuals on it in non-political areas. This leads to the formulation of a discourse that both represents a paradigm for describing situations and entails numerous presuppositions about social reality. Sally Engle Merry (2006:108) notes that people's recourse to human/fundamental rights in order to voice their position "reshape[s] subjectivities in important ways", due to its "capacity to define identity and establish the rights and duties of various statuses, [...] to include and exclude, constituting identities and marginalities". She goes on by saying that the rights talk "include[s] multiple ways of defining selves and, as they become part of local consciousness, produc[es] new subjectivities" (Merry 2008:108). In encompassing and proposing a range of identity models, the jargon of rights connects in a positive way a group's/person's identity and the community they inhabit, by framing their position through the *universalization* of a form of living. In other words, rights provide a standard for expressing one's position, which is no longer only *one's own*, but turns into a role, a position that *everybody* is invited to assume – a position that has its stable place in the social world. This delineation implies a series of assumptions about the very identity that comes to be enshrined in the law. The outlining of a standard position not only draws a map of standard patterns of behaviours, but provides, with and within it, insights of possible interactions, situations and solutions inherent to positions themselves and derived directly from the way in which this position is crafted. In short, a certain formulation of a right will frame the question addressed by it in a given manner, to the extent that the legal articulation of a question will, in turn, shape and influence the public recognition of that very question.[36] The recourse to the language of rights allows tackling issues but does so at the price of favouring one and only one reading of them, from which follows that the right-holder (who is no longer the plaintiff but can be everyone who recognizes herself or her condition to fall under the right) might take on the popularized language of rights for expressing and articulating her situation. Meanwhile, the circulation of rights talk compels states to confront with a scattered multitude of single social actors who lodge claims to see their rights legitimated. On account of this, the state is forced either to ratify the claims raised or to succumb to supranational decisions that would presumably be affirmed by courts.[37]

This far-reaching "juridification" of the political (see Croce 2018) saturates the social realm and urges the individual to constitute herself through a framework of meanings drawing from a specialized context. The separation between politics and rights tends to accommodate the needs of the most part of

36 See the examples offered in West (2011:721, 724, 742).

37 An instance of such a mechanism can be found in the 2015 sentence of the ECHR: *Oliari and Others v. Italy*. Here marriage and the *right* to a family is portrayed as a *human right*. Available online at http://hudoc.echr.coe.int/eng?i=001-139860#{"itemid":["001-139860"]} (last accessed on 25 October 2018).

"actually existing cosmopolitan citizens", by granting them some forms of protections or entitlements. Nonetheless, such an implementation does not take into account the backlash of single, private-oriented decisions, let alone the fact that this form of public protection is issued on the basis of an abstraction that, in relying on a broad generalization, neglects particular or exceptional needs. Therefore, West (2011:714) appropriately highlights that millennial rights, while improving the social condition of those who embrace and reflect standards of normality, end up being detrimental to subordinate and discriminate people.[38] Rights, in supporting an individualized, private view of the political, and in delineating an impenetrable intimate sphere, "do almost nothing to address, and indeed do quite a bit to further insulate, the subordination [of marginalized ones]" (West 2011:714).

38 On the question of normality in its statistical sense, see Haslanger (2015). For a detailed explanation and reflection on how it is possible to "embrace" a standard of normality, that is, how it is possible to become conform to a norm, see in particular Butler (2000, 2004), Serrano (2013).

5 Legal looping effect

The critical reconstruction offered above described the trend that in the last decades led law to a progressive inclination towards an idea of rights based on identity and that adopt and deploy a characteristic jargon – the one of entitlements and privileges. This is well exemplified by policies and legal measures designed to accommodate demands and needs of identity groups, as in the case of laws and policies concerning LGBT rights, based on the category-protecting model – whether protective or extensive. More than in other cases, identity groups reveal the constructedness of social categories and their reliance on a cluster of naturalized assumptions. Labels such as "the homosexual" are not anchored to an alleged essential core (as, for instance, occurs for ethnic or religious groups, in which affinity is attached to supposed natural assumptions – that are not contingent on, and precede, the individual), but derives directly from the essentialization of conducts. In these latter cases, some types of identities come into being when a specific sort of acts gets to be taken as an indication of a kind of person (see Hacking 1986). As Davide Sparti (2001:333) points out, this "classifying process takes place where the verbs are taken over by names: the individual who drinks a lot becomes an alcoholic, the individual who establishes relationships with people of the same-sex, a homosexual". People engaged in specific conducts are "relocated" in identity categories, so much so that certain performances dismiss their temporary, contingent nature and grow into totalizing "profiles", condensed in what Ian Hacking calls "human kinds".

As I will explain in more detail below, human kinds are dynamic classifications, whose two poles are the social world and the subject. The social world is the site of a perpetuation of an incessant taxonomic work, where the emergence of identity categories is the result of an intersection of different technical and technological efforts: legal, medical, economic and theoretical studies contribute to producing classifications of human kinds. Subjects experience on their own skin such classifications, as they are implicitly or explicitly, drawn to embrace them and, subsequently, to frame their way of living in accordance with those prearranged kinds. Nonetheless, the relation between these two poles does not stop here, since by embracing a social classification, subjects become exponent of their human kind. And this is why, in entering the category, their conducts assume a high relevance in the classification itself. To put it bluntly, it is possible to say that, in this framework, members' individual performances and behaviours are doomed to broaden, amend or alter the knowledge about the kind to which they are associated, in such a way that they will affect the features of the very same category.

Human kinds are the only class in which the object classified is shaped by and, in its turn, shapes the classifier:

> [The social context provides] concepts that frame the self-understanding and intentions of the constructed agent. In cases like this, agents incorporate (often consciously) socially available classifications into their intentional agency and sense of self; but as their self-understanding evolves, the meaning of those classification evolves with them. This forms a "feedback loop" (hence the term "interactive kinds") between what we might think of as objective and subjective stances with respect to the classification. (Haslanger 2012:124)

What takes place is a process of "feedback loop" or, to use Hacking's words, "looping effect", which involves a reciprocal interaction between concerted operations of classification and classified agents. There must be an interaction, since the promotion of stable identities – which entails standards of normality and rules of conducts – is contingent on a broad acceptance and an uncritical use of such labels by people. In this light, the imposition of certain compulsory ways of living, as well as the implementation of specific forms of government do not need invasive interventions, but eventuate in a partial forclusion, that leads to select some traits as relevant for the social group and elicit others. In other words, socially visible and accepted categories – while asserting a system of norms about "what to be an X" is – remove and conceal other ways of performing X.

In this chapter, I will draw my attention on every single passage of the process outlined so far: from the emergence of human kinds, to the constitution of identities, up to the analysis of interactive categories and their implications. Central in this phase of my exploration will be how the instantiation of social taxonomies revolving around "human kinds" is conducive to the production of a shared knowledge that, while informing, shapes. To put it another way, the study of specific phenomena, the codification of types of identities and the production of a stable set of data about them allows the exercise of a control over the social world (no matter how diffuse and impersonal). The possibility of grasping the qualities and features of determinate conducts and of crystallizing them into non-negotiable discrete identities is directly connected with the possibility of predicting (and, thus, regulating) them. This process, as will become clearer in the course of this chapter, echoes the one through which legal identities that constitute the subject of millennial rights come into being.

Although the production of social classifications is a stable trait of human sociality and related knowledge production processes (see Douglas 1987), Hacking concentrates on the dynamics of looping effect that characterize the development of specialized knowledges between the 19th and the 20th century. In this period, the massive effort to gain knowledge on human behaviours led to the constitution of an unprecedented wealth of data, based on new techniques, such as statistics, analyses and – more generally – practices of counting. Researchers and theorists became "obsessed with analyse morale, namely the statistic of deviance" (Hacking 1986:161). In order to acquire the broadest comprehension of problematic behaviours, investigations began to be conducted by applying the model of natural sciences:

> We want laws precise enough to predict what individuals will do, or how they will respond to attempts to help them or to modify their behaviour. [...] Only one kind of causality is deemed relevant: efficient causation. One event brings another. (Hacking 1995a:352)

To achieve this aim, the examination of scattered acts proves insufficient. The creation of a reliable body of knowledge entails the discovery of a uniform entity to be studied, something that might lump together scattered acts and provide the basis for a predictive understanding of individuals conducts. Consequently, the learning process concerning human life has, first of all, to provide an object of knowledge (the "doer") as the platform to organize a generalization of her tendencies (the "deed") and the consequent explanation of her habits in accordance with a causational paradigm. "Personal inventories", which stem from this explanatory pattern, produce a set of (allegedly) scientific, abstract and manageable identities, which did not exist "until the practice of counting them came into being" (Hacking 1986:161).

Once those identity categories have come into existence, they undergo a twofold development. On a broader ("social") level, human kinds are crafted by experts, who supply them with a (continually updated) series of descriptions about standards and norms of conduct. On a narrower ("individual") level, they mark the perimeter of assumable identities: human kinds provide subjects with available "ready-made" ways of being and patterns of conduct. It is worth noting that, generally speaking, the possibility itself of embracing an identity is intrinsically related to the accessibility of a category, that is, to the opportunity of figuring out an identity as well as its boundaries and habits, tendencies and characteristics. The added value of the classificatory process – whose creative force is crystallized in the act of recognizing a category by naming it – resides precisely in the opening up of new horizons. Discourses and classifications provide the gamut of available identities, which are rendered intelligible and recognizable by the distribution of detailed knowledge about them. This increasingly growing knowledge is a powerful tool, since in "reorganizing the cognitive frames which rule our classification of social reality" (Sparti 2001:344), it creates the conditions for reframing one's own life experience. New categories produce a new cluster of descriptions, one that could not be accessed before the category itself was created. When a subject – an agent – employs the knowledge produced and its semantic apparatus, she develops into a new self, for, as Sparti (2001:337) puts it, "before certain categories emerge – before a description becomes available (hence before a given classification is made) – it simply is not possible to be recognized as acting (intentionally) under that description". The delineation of an identity christens a modus vivendi, creates connections between kinds, enables a subject to partake in a system in which multiple and variegated powers interact and places her in a structure of non-predictable, but yet expectable, relations. Beyond offering a range of accessible identities, the "search for human kinds", as Hacking (1995a:360) explains, "is inextricably intertwined with prediction and reform".

Thus, the starting point of the looping process is the social inquiry into human kinds. In spite of its being presented as a simple procedure of data collection, such an inquiry does not only lead to the compilation of an archive of information but goes much further. Knowledge concerning social categories draws the map of all cognizable and recognizable identities and does so by providing guidance on the social value of each of them. In other words, the creation of human kinds ends up operating reflexively on subjects, both through the ratification of a finite number of identities and through the assessment of behaviours, so as to dispose them into hierarchies. In short, human kinds ratify both how one is to be an X and what one ought to do as an X.

In discussing what he calls the "making up of people", Hacking pays particular attention to the way in which new categories are forged. He insists that the creative process does not entail the discovery of a problem, an incongruence "that lurked about in nature" (Davidson 2001:21), but rather involves the arbitrary gathering of motives and personal traits under a cohesive group label. Classifications are conceived in to suit the need for explicatory patterns. In this sense, the whole process can be regarded as a "functional understanding" of problematic realities. As I have already mentioned, identities allow recognizing the bearer of "odd" traits, so as to cope with the deeds by dealing with the doer. What is interesting, though, is that the doer herself benefits from an identification that generates a coherent self. She finds her unity along the line of a trait, which becomes decisive in the determination of who she is and on what her social location has to be. Given that, the effectiveness of such forms of regulation is enhanced by people's own inclination to conform spontaneously to the crafted categories, that is, to use them both for narrating their own experience and for labelling that of other people. Such tendency towards self-ascription derives precisely from the combination between the delineation of the boundaries of intelligibility and the fact that such an operation builds on the inscription of moral values in each of the available categories.

The functioning of human kinds might be seen as working along a series of displacements. The first occurs in the transition from the act to the actor. The second consists of a change in the nature of the stigma, which morphs from an intimate condition into an institutionalized one. Institutionalization entails the "publicization" of the stigma, with the consequence that it loses any "personal" connotation and gets singled out as an object of shared (somehow scientific) knowledge. The passage from a social, physical control of abnormal and potentially dangerous subjects to their medicalization (which can be understood as a "technical" control) yields a different connection between the subjects in question and implicitly imposed norms. In this context, the attachment of a stigma appears as no longer arbitrary, in that it is the effect of the discovery of a certified fault. Control is thus re-enacted under the form of therapy at a personal level, and simultaneously takes the shape of a subtle regulation of daily practices. The "management of life" is carried out through the implementation of broadly diffused "re-skilling and re-integrating procedures" (Sparti 2001:333). This makes harsher methods of control unnecessary, as well as it makes unnecessary the exclusion or the "casting out" of problematic individualities from a sociable framework. This means that the management of life encourages smoother techniques of domestication. Society "tends to reclassify and 'take care' of individuals who do not respect its classification repertoire [...] [i]n order to institutionalize forms of recognition and to bring individuals back into shared social identities" (Sparti 2001:333). Here the displacement occurs by means of a universalization of the pathologized trait. At the level of everyday life, the aim is not to correct an X in the here and the now, but to reach – and discover, and tame – all possible Xs, including the Xs-to-come. Control is not exerted on someone but infuses the social realm with a view to persuading everyone about the need of self-regulation; which is to say, one is urged to be the primary controller of one's own conformity with social standards.

Finally, a further form of displacement can be observed in an additional and inverse glide from the general to the particular, or, better, from the medical/scientific impartiality of the ascription to a new moralization of the humankind. In fact, despite their naturalized allure, ratified categories relapse in a compulsory affirmation of cultural norms and standards of living, to the extent that human kinds carry with them the heavy burden of moralization. The pathologization of the stigma involves only superficially a mitigation of the social pressure inflicted on problematic subjects. This is because the "regular attempt to strip human kinds of their moral content by biologizing or medicalizing them" (Hacking 1995a:367) does not lead to a thorough neutralization of their moral contents. Human kinds maintain a bifid nature: on the surface, scientific detachment is their hallmark, but deep down they are still "laden with values". The regulatory impact of human kinds turns out to be particularly effective. For it emerges out of a combination between the abstract scientific rhetoric that surrounds them and the moralizing force that backs them up. Because of this, categories' compelling power is at one and the same time imposed on and chosen by the subjects. The moral implication of being socially labelled as a member of a category exerts its effects on one's self-perception as well as on the subject's "ambience". The medicalization of categories exceeds any scientific diagnosis and involves an ethical judgement about the subject.

Nevertheless, in Hacking's account, it is by exerting effects at the level of personal feelings and self-perception that human kinds acquire weight and significance in people's lives. The ascription to a specific kind affects the overall condition of the subject, who will not only reframe her past and present in compliance with the knowledge about her situation but will also be inclined to fulfil social expectations by (both deliberately and unconsciously) acting in accordance with the standards of the category.

The analysis of these four moments of displacement allows me to highlight the reasons under the considerable impact of human kinds on identity formation. Namely, I will indicate and examine three main factors behind the authority exerted by imposed classifications.

First, once studies begin to be conducted at a specialized, technical level, their results tend to be considered at one and the same time as trustworthy and inaccessible. The more representations of identity features are presented as entities given in nature, the more valuable their scientific account will be deemed (see Foucault 2002:xxi–xxiv).

Second, such a systematization has an impact on the cultural perception of kinds. The production of a classificatory system is instrumental in supporting regulations targeted at problematic conducts. The constitution of human profiles and the mapping of identities offer an overview of interpersonal relations and provide elements for organizing and intervening on the social world. While the former factor leads to the establishment of inflexible norms of conducts, the latter entails the creation of compelling standards of normality and patterns of behaviour. The distinction between "norms of conducts" and "standards of normality" (in the particular sense that I attribute to them in this context) resonates the one between nature and normality. Norms of conduct that emerge out of classificatory schemes are believed to be essential rules pertaining to certain species: they are inscribed in one's own nature and follow from it; they are universal and resistant to change. On the other hand, standards of normality incorporated by these classificatory schemes are the vehicle for cultural expectations regarding inclinations and dispositions of certain kinds. These are claimed to proceed from the natural structure of reality, and yet have a certain degree of ductility, if only because they are usually connected to the spatial and temporal context where they come into being.

The third factor stems directly from the first two, since it is related to the strong influence that human kinds exert on single subjects. As I claimed above, human kinds shape the boundaries of available social identities. The creation of a category, and the consequent disclosure of notions about it, supplies subjects with a language to describe and understand their own life situations. Moreover, since human kinds emerge in response to difficult social circumstances, the identified categories cater for those who suffer from a – still – unnamed pain. In such cases, the classification saturates the scene of the constitution of identities. Newly formed human kinds open up the conditions of possibility for certain subjects to identify themselves and contextualize their anguishes and sense of unease. This form of self-recognition is totalizing as it permeates all dimensions of a subject's life experience, offering relief to those who are confined to an unintelligible position (due to their nonconformity with the standards). In this sense, the bond that connects subjects and kinds derives from the acquisition of a narrative apparatus that allows people to offer a coherent representation of themselves within the social world. People's acquiring an identity amounts to them finding a place, to them being addressable and recognizable (even in an uncanny way). It amounts to people achieving a ratified position in the web of social relations. This is why people "classified in a certain way tend to conform to or grow into the ways that they are described" (Hacking 1995b:21).

Hacking's theoretical apparatus successfully overcomes the flaws that affect a very common view of the construction and imposition of social categories. His dynamic explanation of human kinds opposes that perspective that can be referred to as the paradigm of interpellation. In particular, that view that can be traced back to Butler's concept of the discursive formation of the subject (see infra Chapter 3 and Butler 1997a). In fact, the interpellation paradigm risks concealing a crucial aspect of the looping effect of human kinds, that is, the active role played by the subjects as they identify themselves with a kind.

If interpellation portrays the constitution of identities as a top-down movement from the abstract kind to the single individual, the theory of human kinds takes into account the possibility that a subject might grow into that way of being addressed modifies the direction of this movement. Unlike the paradigm propounded by Louis Althusser and reinterpreted by Butler (1993, 1997a, 1997b, 1997c; Butler and Venditti 2014), Hacking foregrounds a social process of identity formation in which the subject herself acts back on social categories, "so that the classifications and descriptions have to be constantly revised" (Hacking 1995b:21). To be more precise, in Althusser's model, one's becoming a recognizable subject is conditional upon one's subjecting oneself to a form of external recognition (in this sense, he speaks of "*assujettisement*"). To exemplify this process, he describes a scene of interpellation where a policeman hails a passer-by by addressing him with a "Hey you there!". In answering this call, the passer-by subjects herself to such a general interpellation. In this case, the vertical relation between the policeman and the passer-by epitomizes a unidirectional situation whereby identity is foisted upon the subject. The position of the latter depends entirely on the acceptance of an objectified, pregiven social role. Such a description seems not to take into account the outcomes that the embodiment is likely to determine on the imposed categories. It is precisely by turning his attention to this passage – what happens after one takes on an identity – that Hacking unearths the circularity of human kinds.

By devoting special heed to the way in which kinds come into existence, Hacking places his inquiry, from the very beginning, in a precise dimension. His aim is to examine a social mechanism that cannot be restricted to a single moment (the "conferral" of an identity) but has to be positioned in a broader system. In taking as a starting point the constitution of human kinds and in pinning the constitution of identities on the creation of a body of knowledge, Hacking commits himself to an analysis that exceeds the formation of single social actors. Therefore, in moving beyond the subjective moment of socialization, he draws our attention to the recursive impact that single actors have on human kinds:

> To create new ways of classifying people is also to change how we can think of ourselves, to change our sense of self-worth, even how we remember our own past. This in turn generates a looping effect, because people of the kind behave differently and so are different. That is to say the kind changes, and so there is new causal knowledge to be gained and perhaps, old causal knowledge to be jettisoned. (Hacking 1995a:370)

This does not mean that social life is constantly exposed to change, as the process of consolidation of kinds always ensues personalization. In other words, as agents take on fixed, predesigned roles, they are subjected to that category, but at the same time they get to master and actualize it. Once embodied, however, the role becomes the agent's identity. And, even if embracing standards and interiorizing conducts is a necessary process for acquiring an identity, every single performance will overstep, misrepresent, mess up with and loosen the boundaries of the identity model.

Hacking (1995a:380) calls "self-ascriptive kinds" those categories that are accepted and actively employed by members of a group. By consciously embracing the proposed role and the features that it covers, actors play a pre-eminent role in the formation and modification of the body of knowledge concerning their group. As it is the case with all human kinds, self-ascriptive ones are crafted by gathering disparate knowledges (the "fundamental codes of a culture" and "the scientific theories or the philosophical interpretations", as Foucault [2002:xxii] puts it) that, when becoming publicly accepted, are taken up by members of the category themselves. What is crucial in the dynamic game of ascription and self-ascription is that actors deliberately employ the labels used for addressing them. Hacking underscores how this appropriation introduces unexpected variables in the process of identity construction, whose balance of forces gets radically altered. The author deems self-ascriptive kinds to emerge only later in the production of the body of knowledge regarding human beings. In his reconstruction (which centres on the specific temporal and spatial context of the West in the 19th and 20th centuries) from the 19th century, human kinds "were formed on two axes": those of the moral sciences, modelled after natural kinds, and of bureaucratic-statistical practices. This system rests on the sharp division between the knowledge and the known, whose relation takes a stable form, in which the latter is mainly passive vis-à-vis the former. During the second half of the 19th century, the attitude of the "objects of knowledge" changed and a third axis was added. Namely, the subjects (actors) take charge of the description attached to them, using it as an identity label. They recognize themselves in the label and overtly claim to belong to it. In doing so, individuals assume an active role in the creation of knowledge about their own situation, leaving behind their passive role. From this position, actors start to participate to the creation of a body of knowledges, negotiating features and characteristics of a category.

They demand the right to speak for themselves, to shape the knowledge around their own human kind.

On this account, Hacking suggests that the act of self-ascription fosters a replacement of imposed "pejorative labels". It marks the transition from a negative moral connotation of specific categories, which usually involves a silencing of the category and its relegation in the private sphere, to the admission in the public domain. The re-appropriation of a name actively modifies the category's value and the position of its member in the social fabric. Imposed identities, once embraced, turn into sites of collective recognition, which is achieved both at an internal and an external level.

The acquisition of social visibility constitutes the first step to gain a form of political agency that goes beyond the unaware participation in the looping circle of human kinds. This gives the opportunity of being included in the public arena: the self-ascriptive moment might allow for the formation of "pressure groups", "whose aim", to say it with Steven Seidman (1993:106), "is less 'the end of domination' or 'human liberation' than the creation of social spaces that encourage the proliferation of pleasures, desires, voices, interests, modes of individuation and democratization". Hacking provides a straightforward example of self-ascriptive kinds by referring to gay and lesbian movements that reached a peak in the last decades of the 20th century. Even if the example is by now classic, the history of these movements provides the basis for an intriguing and far-reaching analysis of self-ascriptive kinds.

It should be noticed that the constitution of a further pole of acquisition of knowledge around a human kind does not eventuate in an alteration of the effects produced. To put it another way, the mechanism that operates in the standard looping effect of human kinds is reproduced (somehow duplicated) in the case of self-ascriptive ones. The self-management of the group's public image and the circulation of self-crafted standards reproduce the outcomes imposed by externally produced knowledge:

> To simplify overly much, the label 'homosexual' was a term in its original sites applied by the knowers to the known. However, it was quickly taken up by the known, and gay liberation was the natural upshot. One of the first features of gay liberation was gay pride and coming out of the closet. It became a moral imperative for people of the kind to identify themselves, to ascribe a chosen kind-term to themselves. That way they also became the knowers, even if not the only people authorized to have knowledge. [...] We are experiencing a wholly new type of looping effect, when so many of the kinds claim rights to their own knowledges. (Hacking 1995:381)

Hacking highlights how in the development of such movements a constitutive alteration occurs. If the first consequence of self-ascription is properly a liberation, as it allows the multiplication of the sources of information (Hacking calls it a process of "democratization"), there is another ambiguous outcome. The possibility of self-definition – that marks the overcoming of a subaltern position in the social world – urges the members of the category to embrace the constituted identity. In the case of gay people, coming out of the closet and claiming their belonging to the homosexual community is the main strategy to hold their place in the ranks of the "authorized knowers". However, the "moral imperative" to act in accordance with a given trend reproduces the situation experienced by those people who were unwillingly ascribed to a humankind.

Indeed, the participation of multiple "voices" to the delineation of a category carries out a "wholly new type of looping effect" (Hacking (1995a:381–382)). However, this "revolution" occurs only at a superficial level, as it keeps unaltered the complex dynamic of identity formation. More precisely, self-ascriptive kinds set in motion the "looping effect of human kinds", supporting the system of designation and definition of identities, which is based on the conjunction of compelling imposition, assimilation and identification. Based on that, self-ascription does not have to be seen as a disruptive political practice but represents a more fluid occurrence of the social making of human categories.

Nonetheless, the introduction of a variable (that is, the proliferation of poles of knowledge) in the process of constitution of categories opens up a series of possibilities that were precluded in a less flexible system. For this reason, self-ascriptive kinds raises many questions at a theoretical level. Indeed, this form of self-subjectivation – only possible in the relation with an external power – brings up the issue of how intentionality and agency can interfere with broader societal dynamics and collective practices. But it also involves issues of recognition and self-determination. If in order to attain political agency, social actors have to be recognized, what role does intentionality play in the process of identity formation? How do individual acts affect the social world when they are so deeply linked with social ratification? Do self-ascriptive kinds promote a proliferation of nonconforming identities or just pursue a further absorption of differences?

In order to answer these questions, the process of self-ascription has to be inquired in its connection with the political, the social and the legal spheres. To acquire this comprehensive perspective, I will integrate Hacking's account with an analysis of what I believe is a crucial step of the looping effect. Which is to say, the role played by the law in the production of identity categories that emerges out of the social and acts back on it after the transition in the legal field. In doing so, I would like to thematize the shift whereby those that Hacking defines as categories created by experts become legal concepts. While Hacking seems to overlook this shift insofar as the range of experts to which he refers comprises a variety of figures both in the scientific and in the juridico-political spheres, giving an account of it allows to make sense of the way subjects actively contribute to the production of specifically legal concepts, by being involved in the legal discourse in a variety of ways.

First, however, we need to understand the results of the instantiation of a category in the legal sphere, since it always entails a displacement from the category from its original context. Nestled in the legal text, the category is relocated on a level whose rules and meanings differ from the ones at work in the social world. The incorporation of a category into the legal text through legislation or litigation (depending on the procedures the different legal systems provide for) is a process that can be loosely called "juridification". Human kinds that undergo this process acquire a new status and are reallocated in the circle of the looping effect after being importantly modified. In a way, no longer do they constitute a simple part of the flow described by Hacking (knowledge, conducts, new knowledge), but become a hurdle, as it were, in the feedback loop.

Juridified human kinds are given such an eccentric position for three main reasons. First, they are crafted in a technical and, to a greater or lesser degree, proceduralized way. Second, they are vested with special authority. Third, they engage in a relation with social actors which is not reducible to the one described by Hacking.

The first reason has to do with the higher degree of arbitrariness that the crafting of a category by legal experts presents in comparison to the scientific production of knowledge. This is not due to the intrinsic uncertainty that affects the objects of social science, but to the special function that law plays within society. Certain features of the categories are selected for them to be put in the legal text, with a view of implementing particular policies and achieving particular aims. Juridification is at one and the same time the product of, and the drive for, the construction of an exhaustive and saturating definition of identity groups. Haslanger (2012:113–138) understands this process as unfolding along three stages, namely, "selection", "naming" and "ratification". The selective stage coincides with the moment in which discriminatory social relations and their components are detected and isolated. This first stage is heavily dependent upon naming, since it is precisely in the act of "being christened" that a category is made tangible in the eyes of the law. Ratification ensues the delineation and the definition of categories. Thus, this third stage represents the key passage in the juridification of a human kind. According to Haslanger, whereas the tracking of "a group of individuals" and their identification with "a social category" (Haslanger 2012:132) characterizes the formation of human kinds at any level, ratification is a typical trait of the legal incorporation of categories. It represents a threshold, or better, a turning point that changes the status of human kinds by removing them from their original context.

While the emergence of human kinds in the social realm is characterized by a fundamental fuzziness, related to the ongoing evolution of identity categories (which are inevitably exposed to a constant flow), the constitution of legally sanctioned identity categories provokes a displacement isolating the category itself from the dynamism of social practices. In doing so, by way of abstraction and generalization, the social position of the category is altered so as to give life to an archetypal fact-type, which has to be well-determined, highly specific and stable. Categories embedded in the law are rendered less permeable to processes of renegotiation and evolution, and thus forestall the looping circle of human kinds.

The arbitrariness involved in legal selection and the promotion of a particular representation of a category within the legal discourse is conducive to the category acquiring a special authority. This is the quintessence of juridification: an extra-legal element morphs into a legal one by establishing a connection with other elements of the legal system. This connection locates the category in a new web of signifiers – rights, benefits, obligations and responsibilities – that ratify its legal value. The novel set of connections gets the category to lose its character of mere identity-space that a subject dwells in. The category becomes a *means to an end*. Once embedded in the law and endowed with a specific power, human kinds cannot be considered as identities embraced by the subject because of a social pressure. Identity categories are no longer the unwitting, almost compelled, homogenizing label that people in the social field use to account for a series of heterogeneous acts they perform for being read as coherent characters and accepted by others. Nestled in the legal sphere, human kinds become a tool of empowerment.

If we look back to Hacking's human kinds and compare them with the substance of self-ascriptive juridified ones, a basic difference emerges. Socially ratified identity categories constitute, first and foremost, a way to neglect one's own deviance from the norm (through what can be called "a passive embracement") insofar as the subject complies with moral pressure and/or medicalization. In this case, the subject accepts to be described as the member of a problematic category, since this is the only way to turn a socially discriminated position into a socially tolerated one. In doing so, the subject accepts to wield the stigma that the label implies for gaining access to a form of social recognition. On the contrary, self-ascription is a way to claim the rightness of one's own position and to claim for the right to inhabit a nonconforming space. Juridification paves the way for an "empowerment through law". In its turn, empowerment opens up to a politics of negotiation that contributes to the creation, definition and redefinition of human kinds. Self-ascription gives voice to subjects while legal rights make room for this voice to be heard and to connect to the experts' voice in such a way that experts become more and more alert to the view of laypeople. In this sense, self-ascription cannot be considered a path to liberation (see Jay and Young 1992), for it channels an emancipatory tendency that endorses and replicates the very same lexicon of the structure it challenges. This means that self-ascription does not lead to the liberation from a matrix or the disposal of it. Through self-ascription, members of a category gain access to this matrix and affect it by enacting a form of re-appropriation (Croce 2015a; 2015c; Swennen and Croce 2015). The ambiguous nature of the law plainly comes into light: by performing practices of self-ascription, social actors recognize the force of the law and, by doing so, put themselves in the position to ratify a series of imposed norms and crystallize their social position.

The dynamics of self-ascription I have briefly described provides evidence that the law unfolds within the social world by ordering it in accordance with a specific grammar. Self-ascription to a legal category aims at operating with it, through it and in it. It entails the willingness to articulate one's own identity in accordance to the rationality of the law. The reconceptualization of the law, and within the law, throws light on those social entities that were not comprehensible because they fell outside the legal grid of intelligibility, before the law provided a legal category for them. In this way, the law habilitates new ratified categories by conferring relevance and authority on their practices. Yet, in doing so, juridification exerts a special power on categories: legal experts legitimate categories and endow people with privileges, but let no leeway for them to intervene on the category, that loses its malleability and elasticity once engraved in the law.

While my analysis so far makes sense of today's growing success of legal rights as a means to a political end, it also brings into light the connection between rights and juridification. Legal texts, legal experts and the social actors (who have been allowed entry into the legal field) bring into existence a "microcosm" (Croce 2015b) governed by a specific grammar which reflects, but does not mirror, ordinary social life. In this microcosm, social entities, and the web of social relations they give life to, get absorbed by the law and thus take on a different connotation. In this framework – which is steadily becoming a dominant one in the global legal scenario – a triangulation is produced in which social dynamics, once juridified, acquire genuinely political contours. The very moment they enter the legal sphere, social entities become political devices, that is, become capable of modelling the legal sphere so as to broaden its horizons by imposing themselves as legally recognizable entities. The law turns into the powerful vehicle that links the governed and governors (Spanò 2013). This circularity marks the political praxis which inevitably takes the shape of a domesticated dissent or strategic use from within (Halley 2010).

The path towards what can be called a "politics of juridification" (Croce 2018) is perfectly displayed in the change whereby pressure groups have taken over the role of social movements. Pressure groups, along with less-structured social movements, promote actions instrumental in improving the situation of their members. Groups of this sort try to influence the social context in which they operate by pursuing a series of strategies at a legal level and at a cultural one. Insofar as these groups strive to achieve tangible results on both levels, their priorities diverge. Social movements are more concerned with the accomplishment of a deeper cultural change (that might also be likely to bring about a modification in the civic rights system), while pressure groups rather push for a modification of the legal system with an eye to changing the cultural position of their members in the wake of legal recognition. Both pressure groups and social movements are still active in EU and US countries. However, the former are gaining momentum and incrementally acquiring power in decisional processes (Ravitch 2003). This is due to the fact that pressure groups are perceived as a more effective form of political engagement because they are based on the dexterous use of the grammar of law (and particularly the jargon of rights), on the definition of clear-cut targets (attainable within a reasonable period of time), and on a tendency to "sectorialization". On the contrary, social movements take up struggles that involve vaster forms of mobilization and gather together a broader variety of instances, channelling their requests in less formal actions and endorsing a form of political protest whose possibilities of success are insecure. Also Moya Lloyd (2007) speaks of social movements as contexts of collective engagement operating within the frame of socio-historically determinate conditions. Social movements constitute unstable groups, whose actions take place in an opaque social sphere where negotiation is not only a dispute between emergent social realities and political institutions, but a broader struggle among several actors (see e.g. Goldoni 2014). We can see how this type of social mobilization tends to be based on a critique "from outside", that propounds non-compliance as its main form of dissent. While "sectorialization" and "juridification" are common currency in pressure groups' strategies, that of social movements is a push for "culturalization" and the creation of spaces of social visibility by means of non- (or not-necessarily) juridified actions that are brought to bear on the political sphere.

The main difference between these two modes of political engagement has to do with the way claims are raised and the frame they are given. While social movements aim at creating the conditions for a social shift, pressure groups accord pre-eminence to legal means, as their claim-making relies on institutionalized procedures (mainly of a legal type, even in civil law countries). Both, however, seek to exert a transformative potential on the social worlds and its normative repertoire. Because of this, the idea that the possibility of affecting and transforming the conservative, hegemonic structure of society does not necessarily imply lies the rejection of institutionalized procedures – as many commentators strongly contend (see e.g. Duggan 2002; Warner 2000). Indeed, the effectiveness of pressure groups' interventions gives the lies to theories assuming that institutionalization as such hampers the revision of available meaning and practices. The successful activity of pressure groups certifies the porosity of the legal space, which makes room for emerging input and instances. Nonetheless, the effects of the different activity of social movements and pressure groups cannot be equalled. Despite this, when the legal jargon prevails over other forms of political engagement, even if the revision of social meanings and practices is not necessarily inhibited, the iterative power is differently distributed. While in the case of social movements, the production of meanings is handled by indeterminate, fluid, variable sources, in the case of pressure groups, the necessity of conforming to the language of the law profoundly conditions both the structure of the discourse and the way claims are made. Doubtless, the prominence of an institutionalized formality does not result in the establishment of any "sovereign power" that opposes social change. For, the millennial legal authority is exerted through the disposition of a semantic apparatus, rather than through the exhibition of viable alternatives. In addition, legal meanings keep a strong connection with their social counterpart, and, thus, they are never stabilized *a priori* and their meaning is exposed to contestation and revision. Thus, social forces might use and employ the legal jargon even in an oppositional or disruptive way. However, the formal procedures of the legal institutions exert an inhibiting effect at a structural level, impinging on the way in which one can give an account of one's own situation, as well as the mode to couch issues that have always to conform to legal terms.

In short, juridification alters what many authors have referred to as the "iterative process" (see in particular Butler 1990/1999, 1993, 1997a, 1997b), without preventing resignification. The agential force of actors within the legal field is not suppressed, but even enhanced precisely in virtue of an appeal to law. The use of legal means invests social actors with a special authority that gets rid of a conventional view of law as a "sovereign power" precisely because such sovereignty gets diffracted and diffused in ways that "multiply" the law itself (or at least its sources). Nevertheless, even if almost everybody can potentially participate in such a diffracted and diffused authority, the need to acquire such an authority (and to comply with its form) alters the course of iteration.

Similarly, social movements and pressure groups give life to quite different relations between social actors and categories. Social categories which attach to the subject – those categories that social movements aim to challenge in the first place – are exposed to an ongoing process of transformation, or rather, to a potentially endless looping effect. On the contrary, the legal labels are much less flexible and require previous acceptance for actors to make use of them (Swennen and Croce 2015). The political impact of these two modes of engagement is affected by such a relevant disparity. Whereas social movements try to make a given category acceptable and visible by defiantly endorsing the label that denotes it (that is to say, by attaching themselves to a category through the embracement of a label and by performing what this label entails), pressure groups that favour institutionalized procedures endorse a label with no intention to mobilize its symbolic force and to challenge the assumptions and beliefs on which it is premised.

Based on this juxtaposition, we can see that the tendency for culturalization as a means for political change, that characterizes social movements, proves unnecessary in the perspective of pressure groups. Far-reaching collective strategies are abandoned in favour of an approach that privileges the pursuit of well-determined and context-specific aims. Pressure groups try to achieve specific goals through legal means in such a way that social actors gather around sectional interests and their alliance becomes contingent upon the action they are momentarily performing. These coalitions are inherently transitory (or at least linked to a specific temporality) and pursue definite objectives, which have to be achieved in a reasonable lapse of time. Interests (often expressed in terms of injunctive or compensatory redress mechanisms) constitute the genuinely political feature of these judicial procedures, which do set in motion political change, and yet make room for political enclaves to mobilize a fragmented politics of change on the basis of a particularistic logic.

It is precisely the rationality underlying the activity of pressure groups that inadvertently brings into question the concept of political representation. On the one hand, the creation of specific groups raises the issue of who the members of these groups are. By naming themselves, pressure groups lay a claim to the right to represent a collective, with the consequence of creating an unwitting flattening, one that expunges potentially dissenting viewpoints (Halley 2001, in particular 41–42). LGBT groups provide a clear example: under a very broad label several political streams are unified, so much so that "conservative" gays find themselves (at least "on paper") struggling side-by-side with "left" radical and queer activists (NeJaime 2003). Such a levelling has a high impact on the social representation of the category itself, since it "can be interpreted as a wholesale shift toward the pursuit of inclusion within those institutions [...] [previously] regarded as sites of oppressions" (Croce 2015a:11). Problematic human kinds try to adapt to social standards so as to gain acceptance, despite their nonconforming positioning. In doing so, the "domain of difference" to which single members of the groups belong to "comes to be fragmented into a multiplicity of different domains" (Croce 2015a:12). This levelling results in a layering that creates division inside the problematic category and this produces a further instance of "otherness". Paradoxically identity-based claims which aim at overcoming marginalization enact an even more exclusionary politics that offers representation only for certain portions of the category, at the price of ghettoizing other segments of it (see Gilden 2008; Monceri 2011, 2012; NeJaime 2003; Preciado 2014; Serrano 2013). On the other hand, pressure groups function as a supplementary mediation in the context of a more and more scattered social fabric, which political institutions prove no longer able to represent. In this new representational horizon, the contemporary subject is freed from stable groups of belonging and inhabits several positions at one time. She becomes "interchangeable".

In the face of this transition, political representation is obtained through the formation of pressure groups, that is, through the creation of collectives of people whose cumulative efforts acquire a "dominant" position in the legal process. On one side, representation is gained first and foremost as users of law and on the other, users of law count on this form of representation to gain access to the legal field (Nader 1984, 2002). To fit their new role, social actors undergo a "process that prompts the parties to transcend their personal view of things and to locate themselves into a semiotic framework that transforms [their position in] the conflict" (Croce 2015c:14). On this account, political representation turns into a double-faced institute: a superficial, public one, that is, the image itself of pressure groups; and a deeper one, that is, the representation that the legal officials and those who represent the parties in the legal field provide of the essential characteristics that make the group a group. The type of "political" lawyering that hallmarks this emerging composition between the legal field and political action is, as Gary Bellow (in NeJaime 2003:516–517) puts it, "a medium throughout which some of us with law training choose to respond to the need for change in an unjust world". In this scenario, lawyers become key figures of pressure groups. In determining the strategies to be adopted and the way to frame the objectives, lawyers, as Halley (2000:46) points out, are in the position to "alter the social definition of the group itself". Yet, by altering the social definition, effects are exerted at the level of identity-formation. Under the form of litigation, we can see the juridified version of the looping effect at work and can grasp the ultimate results of the *liaison dangereuse* between human kinds and the current form of the legal sphere.

The case of pressure groups has brought to light the need for social actors to resort to the specialized jargon of law in order to interact with it and gain benefits from this entrance into a legal sphere. Furthermore, it has revealed the high value of a strategic rationality in the political exploitation of one's own identity.

In this context, human kinds cease to be the mark of a social stigma and, once embedded in the law, turn into genuine tools of empowerment. Juridified identities are ratified, recognized and, thus, engraved in the social realm, so much so that self-ascription becomes a way to participate to, claim for and naturally acquire a series of privileges. Indeed, nothing comes for free. The instantiation of a category in the legal sphere modifies the position of the category in the web of social relations. Law vests categories with a special authority but at the same time reduces them to very plain entities, by means of abstraction and generalization. Human kinds then lose the opacity that characterizes them in the social sphere and come to be clearly defined and sharply determined in the process of juridification. Even if it is not completely true that this new contextualization crystallizes the value and the meaning of human kinds, it certainly imposes rules and forges a new path to attaining changes (Coccia 2014:62).

First of all, the incorporation of a human kind in the legal sphere entails an alteration of its "functions". As happens in pressure groups, the assumption of a juridified identity may be contingent on the achievement of a determinate aim. An "actor can use her or his identity to gain 'political standing'" (Bernstein 1997:536), even if the human kind embedded in the law has been "produced" by the recognition of "a social movement in which she or he is not directly implicated" (Bernstein 1997:536). The possibility of taking advantage of a classification without being involved in a cultural collective mobilization places great stress on the individual, purely strategic dimension of self-ascription. As is the case with what Bernstein calls "identity deployment", the strategic use of one category leads to a particular expression of "identity such that the terrain of conflict becomes the individual person so that the values, categories and practices of individuals become subject to debate" (Bernstein 1997:537–538). When this happens, or better, when individual identities emerge in the political arena by making use of legal tools, the horizon of culturalization vanishes almost completely. Identity deployment appears, as Bernstein (1997:537–538) puts it, "as a way to contest stigmatized social identities for the purposes of institutional change".

I would expand her point by stressing the very personal character of this contestation. As it is up to the single person to turn to the law and use it for oppositional goals, I take the notion of "contestation" to be misleading. It seems to me that this term recalls a political and collective form of resistance which is not present in the case I am analyzing here. Identity deployment marks the shift from a politics based on public critique to a politics ingrained in the claim to rights. This is displayed also in the way in which single users approach the law: they are called upon to take a stand on the basis of pregiven categories, proposed by and crafted in the law. In fact, at an initial stage, one's recourse to the law cannot be wholly critical and oppositional. The actor cannot but refer to the models provided by the law in order to challenge them. Only after this original acceptance and self-recognition can the subject operate in and on the legal sphere. But there is something more at stake in making oneself knowable by and through the law. Through the opening up of a place in the law for marginalized categories, a site of political agency is produced; but, the price for the possible achievement of a political agency is the unavoidable request of using the instrument provided by the law. In the social realm, actors face constantly the urgent invitation of the law asking for recognition, transparency, order. Intelligibility is almost compelled on individuals. The opportunity of being recognizable becomes a powerful offer, since it is the persuasive invitation to weigh in politically: "Identity politics suddenly is no longer mere or simple resistance: it begins to look like power" (Halley 2000:43).

In this context, the practice of self-ascription is ignited by the interaction among the exhibition of abstract, crafted identity categories, the adoption of such pregiven ways of being, and the desire for recognition and empowerment, characterized by the acquisition of a "guided" political agency. The poles of the law and the subject are unified by the third element of this triangle, that is, the formation of a political agency which is necessarily shaped under particular conditions. The attainment of it necessitates a "guided" introduction of subjects in the sphere of law. The intercession of experts – mostly, the lawyers, as Douglas NeJaime (2003) clearly remarks – allows the replication and the circulation of the legal lexicon and the incorporation of single subjects within it. The acquisition of a political agency is channelled by the strategic embracement of a social obligation. Empowerment, as Halley would have it, begins to smell like compulsion.

Moreover, if we focus our attention on the level of individual formation, the possibility of adopting a pregiven identity for juridico-political aims paints an unexpected scenario since, the effects of the assumption of a strategic identity exceeds its deployment on the part of single individuals and affect the category itself. In other words, the management of identities in relation to a legally imposed representation is not exempted from the repercussions that are typical of the looping effects of human kinds. The compliance with the law has a backward impact on the subjects who, in embracing a stereotyped role, inadvertently end up taking on all the assumptions implicated in it. We can take the example of transsexual people who decide to strategically portray themselves as suffering from Gender Identity Disorder (in accordance with the definition given in the DSM-4) so as to gain access to sex reassignment surgery (Butler 2004a:75–101). "Patients" decide to manifest and perform the symptoms of GID to gain access to medical procedures and welfare assistance by voluntarily submitting themselves to a positive diagnosis. Even when the subject demonstrates to be "very savvy" about the features she is re-enacting, "the regulatory discourse surrounding the diagnosis takes on a life of its own" so as to gain access to sex reassignment surgery (Butler 2004a:91). The autonomous decision to assume a pathologized identity (which is always counterbalanced by the unintended validation of its parameters) entrenches transsexuality in the medical sphere. The behind the scenes of a canny fulfilment of (juridified) medical parameters reveals the site of a passive submission to a canon. To get advantages out of institutionalized resources, the actor is caught in a system of domination, reproduced by the same subjective exploitation of such resources. In addition to that, the deployment of an identity turns out to be not entirely or "not necessarily a consciously chosen strategy" (Bernstein 1997:536), since the impact it exerts over and beyond the personal moment of choosing has to be ascribed to the impersonal power of the law.

In other words, the lexicon put forward by the law has a grip on the categories it hails, whether or not social actors make use of it.

In summary, the juridification of categories exerts a twofold influence on the social realm, since legal performances carried out by means of a self-ascription results in a proliferation of the legal grammar. This implies the currently growing reinforcement of the legal authority and, above all, its consequent instillation and its rootedness in the social realm. As we can see, the looping mechanism is reproduced here, but its contents change. What circulates in the juridified looping effects is no longer a flowing social discourse weaved between experts and human kinds. After all

> The law is nothing but an effective word, able to shape the human life that it addresses, for the mere fact of its existence and of its enunciation. Living in a society of law, then, means to live in a society that has isolated a number of socially effective words and discourses. It has physically segregated them, it has collected them in a space that is separated from the other social spaces. [...] From a material, linguistic and grammatical point of view this disparate set of words has no peculiar traits: these words differ from the others neither for a particular power, nor for their meaning, nor for a specific poetic virtue. [...] Their special and detached position is thus justified by a set of myths. (Coccia 2014:61–62; author's translation)

This "magic" condition of the legal lexicon brings about the impossibility of governing and controlling the dynamics and the consequences of one's own self-ascription. Under the surface of an empowerment achieved by the deployment of legal means lies the imposition of a "colonizing intelligibility" (Croce 2015b). Legal techniques and grammar define political events by appointing them with a name. What is more, juridification involves not only the alteration of the background conditions of social entities, nor will it be limited to a redefinition of institutionalized identities and relations. Juridification is, most importantly, the production of a finite number of reified social abstractions.

So far, I have argued that juridification reduplicates the looping mechanism to which human kinds are subjected. Through the incorporation of specific categories and by pursuing protective aims, the state acquires a very peculiar authority on the social groups it recognizes. The very act of integration involves a modification of a social group's position and perspectives, which get "mitigated" and modified in accordance with legal requirements. These "strategies tend to enhance state regulation over the issues in question", and their transposition into the legal field "potentially empower[s] the state", which is made capable of "invoking" its own instruments "against the very social movements that pushed for their acceptance as legal doctrine" (Butler 1997b:24). In fact, once categories have been secured in the legal body, they are turned into static, reified entities occupying an eccentric position in the social domain. Members of juridified human kinds lose their primary relation to the language they use to describe themselves and get to make use of a symbolic apparatus that is drawn from a narrower set of options. Basically, the balanced connection between exponents of a human kind and experts' discourses is carved up and channelled through the legal structure that becomes the primary source of authority (as it were, the main pole) of the looping process.

This form of "dispossession" (Butler and Athanasiou 2013), namely the impossibility of "owning" the grammar of the definition, takes the form of a twist that starts in the language and unfolds at many levels. Juridified categories are turned into hardly negotiable labels, whose modification is conditional on official procedures. Social actors find their political dimension only after an inaugural subjection to the law. Then, it is the legal ratification that allows them to become a legitimate pole of the circle of human kinds. Dispossession is doubtlessly a very strong term; nonetheless it vividly depicts the situation produced by the juridification of categories. When a social category enters the legal system, it is much less sensitive to living relationships and daily practices. It comes to be strengthened and supported by an official ratification, regardless of its multiple social connections. In addition, to claim their affinity with the category, those who invoke it have to take on a specialized language and can articulate their subjectivity only through that bounded lexicon.

I have already noted that in order to secure the identification of the members of a juridified human kind (both at a social interpersonal level and at a legal one), experts are pushed to pinpoint their accounts of those categories on a series of rules, statistics and data which permit a univocal recognition. Hence, categories are reframed and generalized in the wake of what appears to be a "legal abstraction". Whilst the value and the need of such a generalization are easily inferable, the very strong impact that they have on a broader, social level is more difficult to spot. Nonetheless, the abstraction proposed at a legal level, as the case of pressure groups shows, interferes with the perception of the category at a social level. The circulation of legal standards results in the naturalization of the model supported by the law. A levelling occurs between the creation of legally determining norms and the validation of naturalized norms of conduct inherent to the category itself. To put it another way, juridification exasperates "a very primitive 'default mode of generalizing'", (which is at work in any classification concerning interactive kinds) "that picks up on significant or striking properties and links them to a psychologically salient kind" (Haslanger 2012:451). In these cases, the legal recognition of an identity category ends up coinciding with a totalizing regulation and an overall management of it. Essentialization occurs when norms themselves come to epitomize an ideal of normality, which in turn radiates assumptions about the nature itself of the protected groups. The descriptive force is "invoked as part of an explanatory project that assumes that some properties are prior to others", so much so that it is rendered into a normative force. It is easy to take a further step:

> Implication and presupposition of this sort become part of the common ground, often in ways that are hard to notice and hard to combat, and they become the background of our conversation and our practices. (Haslanger 2012:468)

The production of a normative structure and the delineation of standards of normality, as Sarah-Jane Leslie (in Haslanger 2014:372) observes, go hand in hand with the postulation of an "inductive generalization" that bears "a certain kind of normative force". In other words, the idea of normality that sprouts from a set of ratified norms around a human kind substantiates a shift from what is taken to be representative of a kind (or what is "statistically" representative of it) to a "metaphysical ground" with which we are pushed to conform:

> The Normative Assumption takes the ideology a step further: Fs being G by nature isn't just how things are, it is how things should be. It is (normatively) normal. We who seek the good should help Fs be G, should regard Fs that are not G as defective and in need of correction. This is key, of course, to marginalization. [...] If the outlier is not normal, then they are not as they should be (they are, or the circumstances are, unnatural) and there is need of correction. If correction is unsuccessful, then they are presumably defective and appropriately marginalized. Substitute for 'black person' in the argument any nondominant group descriptor. The world doesn't always reinforce our judgments of what's natural and right with perfect regularities, but that poses no challenge to an ideology that includes the Normative Assumption. Rather, the world's imperfections provide us opportunities to set nature on its proper path. (Haslanger 2015:389)

In this scenario, the positioning of what Haslanger and Leslie call a "normative assumption" in an isolated and authoritative system, which exerts a strong influence on the social realm (such the legal one), enhances and increases the weight of the postulated norms. From this viewpoint, essentialization is counter-punctual to the fragmentation and the victimization of social groups and is supported by legal strategies implemented by state officials and lawyers – that which, as I will explain below, falls under the rubric of heteronormization.

Fragmentation derives directly from the identification of a univocal identity model. With this term I refer to the process of internal partition of problematic categories. The postulation of a standard establishes a hierarchy in the category. By means of discriminating between a "right way" to be an X and "bad" one. By turning its attention to a specific model (to wit, by reducing a way of living to an identity), the law implicitly favours a model over others. In this way, legal recognition ends up involving only a section of the group, so as to avoid extending protection to other nonconforming members. On one hand, members of marginalized groups who fulfil the legal model might actually take advantage of the application of the extension of rights. But, on the other, all those who fall outside the scope are left with two options: either they comply with the standards or they are exposed to deeper marginalization, one that is characterized by a form of unspeakability. Not only are those who do not meet legal standards deprived of legal representation; no less significantly, they suffer from the lack of an adequate social one, since the legal description, as we have seen, serves as a comprehensive redefinition of the group at a social level. Thus, legal recognition takes the form of an *aut aut*: only those who are willing to make themselves visible have access to the benefits provided by the law. It is worth noting that, to trigger this process, there is no need for policymakers to supply a *stricto sensu* description of the group, because implications and indications of what a group is are contained in the regulative vein of the law. Therefore, fragmentation risks resulting from the conditions set by the law itself. Alternatively, it can take a subtler form and convey a standard by fostering specific ways of living over others, for example through taxation and various policy measures. Same-sex marriage provides an example (by now classic) of this latter case. The extension of marriage to same-sex couples has been considered one way among several others to redeem a position of social disadvantage. However, at a certain point the acquisition of this basic civic right became the flagship of the struggle for recognition as a whole. Marriage was (and in some places still is) one among the many bastions of gay discrimination, and this makes the claim for the right to marry part and parcel of the battle against marginalization. Nonetheless, the very institution of marriage is inherently linked with a series of assumptions which are imbued with traditional values, such as (to mention just a few) monogamy, intimacy, parenting rights. As many authors contend (see e.g. Chasin 2001; Cobb 2011; Edelman 2011; McRuer 2006; Warner 2000), the more the idea of a "respectable gay couple" (polished with marriage) achieved social approval, the more other (same-sex) forms of relationships were refused. The image of the "good gay" (Warner 2000) made its way through the mainstream culture, and obscured, or even effaced, all those realities that do not mirror the "well-behaved, domesticated lesbian [and gay] couples" (McRuer 2006:83). A famous cover of *The Nation* (published the April 21, 1997) bespeaks this fracture in the LGBT community. It "presented readers with an image of two gay men and their cat safely ensconced in their living room" (McRuer 2006:82); the headline read: "Creating a New Gay Culture: Balancing Fidelity and Freedom". This alleged "new gay culture" is based on the idea of "marriage as a social institution [...], in the words of Bishop John Shelby Spong, 'marked by integrity and caring and ... filled with grace and beauty'" and entails the denial of "a culture of 'gay bars, pornography, and one-night stands'". As we can see, the promotion of a style of living inadvertently lays the basis for a promotion of a model that displays how to "normally" be part of a category within society. It is certainly true that the reproduction of the model inscribed in (or prescribed by) the law might always involve the conscious, deft act of self-ascription, but the effects of this re-enactment exceed the boundaries of a controlled exploitation of the legal tools. As the previous section has shown, the circulation of a cluster of discourses about an identity category holds sway over the members of that category in unexpected, unforeseeable ways. Its influence is not limited to the moment of formation of subjectivity, since it will constitute the common knowledge around the category, that is, it will support a general perspective, not limited to the legal field. The broad reception of the canon introduced by the law has an effect on marginalized realities, since it draws a boundary between a tolerated diversity and an inconceivable, outrageous one.

No less relevant is the twofold effect of victimization exerted on the members of juridified groups. The incorporation of a category within the law depends on an "arbitrary" delineation of that very category. This means that the legislator is inclined to give prominence to determinate traits and to exclude others from its definition. Such a definition, then, does not constitute a faithful representation of a social entity, but a representative image of the issue addressed by the law. As a consequence, policies aimed at tackling marginalization highlight, among other things, all the features that "ignite" the discriminated position of the group in the social field. In doing so, juridified categories will retain their connections with the stigma that prompts marginalization. As long as members of a discriminated category enjoy the legal right to use a social stigma in order to overcome their imposed weaknesses, the prejudice against them will be re-instantiated in the social discourse as inherent in that category. The rhetoric of the victim deprives the marginalized subject of her political agency – in perpetuating her "state of minority", (Giglioli 2014) – sanctions her irreconcilable difference from the norm, and forces her to take advantage of an abject position instead of doing away with it. When the law goes down this path, it fosters the improvement of a group's conditions and at the very same time, configures as naturally incapable of participating to social relationships without a legal protection. In this way, policies inspired by this legal trend "tend to consolidate the regulative norms and thus function at odds with challenging those norms" (Brown 2000:234). This is evidence that securing a right does not automatically result in the provision for a different social position. Somehow, the possibility of gaining access to "tailored" legal opportunities can even worsen the social situation of some groups. The legal acquisition of a right might fail to take the form of an increased social power, and this is because "in inegalitarian, orders, rights differentially empower different social groups, depending upon their ability to enact the power that a right potentially entails", which is easily translatable in the formula: "the more social resources the less social vulnerability" (Brown 2000:232).

In addition, laws usually take into account singular fact-types, so that categories benefit from protections that tend to address only one aspect of people's identity. In this sense, not only does the law prove incapable of accounting for the complex web of social interrelations that a subject has to face; but it also condemns marginalized people to rely on a "segmented" form of protection (Brown 2000:235, Crenshaw 1989). Thus, victimization exhibits its character of a schizophrenic enclosure, one that leaves a mark on the subject, but, at the same time, offers a partial remedy for her sufferings. Laws regarding women's rights or gender issues herald such a "subordination through legal empowerment". We can take as an example the legislation concerning maternity leaves in Italy. This topic has been highly debated both in Italy and more in general in the EU. In particular, Italian working mothers gained, in 1971, the right to hold down their job and be re-instantiated after a maternity leave. Since then, they are granted a period of a leave that goes from 2 to 5 months and which can be extended accordingly to each specific situation. On the other hand, paternity leave has been regulated by a law passed in 2012 (L. 92/2012), and the law clearly states that the father can benefit from a paternity leave of three working days. From this very simplified perspective, we can already observe that such dispositions reproduce and reinforce mainstream roles and, furthermore, account for a minimal segment of a working mother's life. With their resolutions, such laws reveal that

> the value of rights language for women is [...] deeply paradoxical: rights secure our standing as individuals even as they obscure the treacherous ways in which that standing is achieved and regulated; they must be specific and concrete in order to reveal and redress women's subordination, yet potentially entrench our subordination through that specificity; [...] they emancipate us to pursue other political ends while subordinating those political ends to liberal discourse; they move in a transhistorical register while emerging from historically specific conditions; they promise to redress our suffering as women but only by fracturing that suffering – and us – into discrete components, a fracturing that further violates lives already violated by the imbrication of racial, class, sexual, and gendered power. (Brown 2000:238)

The paradox, then, is that rights that entail some specification of our suffering, injury, on inequality lock us into the identity defined by our subordination, while rights that eschew this specificity not only sustain the invisibility of subordination, but potentially even enhance it (Brown 2000:232).

The analysis of victimization stresses the connection among rights, prejudices and cultural obstacles. Legal procedures are not exempted from the social biases that weaken marginalized people's positions in the social field and, furthermore, offer a type of support which, in being imposed from above, is not always capable of overcoming a cultural stigma that may remain unaltered in the social, despite specific legal measures.

Finally, "heteronormization" brings about a situation in which social actors, in order to enter the legal field, have to accept and assume the specific grammar of the law. In fact, the premise for any fruitful interaction with the law is the subsumption under its categorial grid, which is the combination of a lexicon, a jargon, as well as a set of explicit and implicit and norms. Given the complexity of the "legal pattern", a deep and sound knowledge of its structure proves crucial in approaching it adequately, above all when the actor aims at changing it or making a strategic use of the legal tools. In this sense, lawyers and legal experts provide indispensable support to those actors who want to (or need to) challenge, modify or amend the law. As we have seen, the isolation of the legal sphere and the key role of legal experts cause an imbalance in the steady looping effects of human kinds within the social realm. Lay people, with their habits and behaviours, might not be able to influence those institutions that regulate certain aspects of their lives. This incapacity derives mainly from the fact that the law has an inevitably unifying and limited perspective. While in the constitution of human kinds, experts have to follow the vaster spectrum of possible changes in a category, juridified human kinds function the other way around: it is the single individual who has to fulfil the description provided by the law in order to fall under it. In other words, while, in the former case, human kinds must fit the purpose of giving an account of the group they are labelling, in the latter, juridified categories define a group in the body of law, with which members are required to accord when they have recourse to it. This means that, in the eyes of the law, "nonconforming" conducts lie outside the juridified category and thus are considered to be irrelevant to the development of the latter. Hence, heteronormization is the consequence of that kind of dispossession which robs social actors of suitable means to exercise their own political agency. Under the individual, subjective, expression of this heteronormization lies the broader question of the relation between law and social practices.

The transmutation that ensues this process is well exemplified in the case of laws concerning same-sex parenting. Robert Leckey (2011a, 2011b) analyzes the contradictions inherent in being a lesbian parent. He avers that the reality of lesbian families moves away from the structure of traditional families (two co-habiting parents, clear roles, well-defined familial settings) as lesbian families with children may comprise a different number of parents, while the biological father can be included as a co-parent or other significant figures may become part of the *ménage familier*. Moreover, traditional kinship terms (such as "mum" and "dad") are substituted for other forms of naming, while duties and tasks, rights and privileges of the members of these "extended families" differ consistently from the ones that characterize heterosexual families. Despite this, the legal response to lesbian parenting seems not to take into account these differences, as it propounds regulations based on conventional models. This means that, despite the actual daily experience of lesbian parents, the law sticks to certain parameters, such as coupledom, familial roles and others. In doing so, the law urges those people who want to take advantage of its benefits to embrace a definite model and fulfil determinate standards. This exhorts those who do not align with such models (but want to enjoy legal recognition) to turn to legal experts who may work in the interstices of the law in order to make their situation fit legal standards. This is evidence that even eccentric practices yield to law's regulatory power and are forced to comply with it. Nonconformity is not an option before the law, if it is true that any appeal to the law involves a form of compliance with its terms and rules. The denial of alternative ways of living that follows from legal regulation constitutes the dark side of heteronormization. Social actors are compelled to meet legal standards in order to be heard and gain legal visibility, so that paradoxically, the acquisition of a right results in the relinquishment of one's own political standpoint:

> As we incessantly refer our political life to the law, we not only sacrifice opportunities to take our inherited political condition into our own hands, we sacrifice as well the chance to address at a more fundamental or at least far-reaching level various troubling conditions which appear to require redress. (Brown and Halley 2002:20)

Nevertheless, the dependence upon legal experts and the observance of imposed norms represent the most superficial aspect of a deeper loss of political autonomy which stems from the juridification of identity categories. In fact, legal constraints infiltrate social practices and exert unintended effects that modify social balances and personal horizons.

6 Difference dissimulated

Politics of marginalities

The analysis carried out so far illustrates the relation between legal measures and the production of classifications focusing on how this relation impacts on the social world and the production of identities. Legal measures and legal techniques are becoming the pillars of an emerging governmental structure that goes beyond the traditional boundaries of the political sphere and, at least in some cases, escapes the reach of "legitimate" political authority. The unforeseen supremacy of a polymorphic and deterritorialized juridical (a multi-headed, diffuse cluster of procedures and instances) substantiates a political scenario marked by an excess (Cooper 1998) that is manifest in the role that laws, judicial rulings and legal practices play in the creation and establishment of a new sociopolitical setting.

This last chapter homes in on the political import of this legal metamorphosis. More specifically, I will look at the relationship that these phenomena bear to political government and political agency by examining the kinds of governing practices that come to mark the current scenario. I will explore three different types of governing techniques that are to be seen in counterpoint to the three policy strategies considered in the first part of this book (Chapters 1–3). A closer inspection into these policies from this point of view will shed light on the similarities and dissimilarities among them. Similarities are important insofar as they provide evidence that all policy strategies (and not only category-protecting ones) are characterized by a general reliance on the paradigm of rights and the production of classificatory schemes. Dissimilarities, on the contrary, will concern the type of governing techniques they unleash.

While earlier in this work I emphasized the particular effectiveness of category-protecting policies and their influence on people's everyday life and ordinary practices, it might seem that this does not apply to the other types of policy, whose ongoing effects prove to be either barely perceived once they have been taken for granted, or brought into question only in restricted circles (such as scholarly or advocacy groups). Despite this, the use of the jargon of rights and the set of values that surround it are by no means a peculiarity of category-protecting policies. In the emerging conjunction of politics and law, all three kinds of inclusive policies tend to develop their strategies with an eye to the model of human/fundamental rights, which generally invokes the celebration of individual entitlement and the promotion of liberal values (autonomy, self-determination, privacy, intimacy).

It is worth looking at similarities in more detail. Two are the main factors that resonate among these inclusive policies. First, their goals and structure are attuned to a language that promotes a vision of law as conferral. Moving away from the modern, contractualist view of the law as an explicit and mutual agreement between the state and the citizen, today's policy models are inclined to supply legal provisions that seem somewhat free from commitments for the addressees. Of course, as Robin West's (2011) analysis emphasizes, such a seeming lack of obligation is misleading, for duties and requirements are concealed under a language that is naturally inclined to accord pre-eminence to entitlements. Speaking of legal rights allows policymakers to duck the thorny issue of the prices of inclusion. In granting privileges, the state claims some privileges for itself: the privileges not to address certain problematic areas of life, not to be engaged in the public promotion of certain measures, not to imagine alternative forms of social relationships and alternative visions of the political community. In other words, the jargon of rights offers the possibility of neglecting the reciprocity of the legal relation, which is conducive to an opaquer management of political strategies, whose costs and requirements come to magically melt and disappear, looming quietly on the social realm.

Second, all these inclusive models rely on a language that heavily affects the way in which they account for discrimination and inclusive practices, impinging on the social and linguistic representation of the marginalized subjects they address. Even as they do not explicitly embrace the rhetoric of "identity policies" take on the construction of specific "human kinds". The way categorization processes are implemented differs from one policy strategy to another, in view of their respective intents. Opportunity-oriented policies produce a type of category apt to bear a definite national identity and its cultural-political marks. In much the same way as the category of the "alcoholic", the "citizen" (who claims her entitlement to the privileges guaranteed by the state legal system) collects a cluster of features outlining a role. While the alcoholic gestures towards an identity that narrates a specific reiterated history (which usually goes from unhappy childhood to shame), the citizen reflects state-based ideologies gesturing towards belonging, tradition and national heritage. Similarly, the "human being", to whom capability-based policies refer, is the concretion of a series of capabilities that go beyond a merely descriptive combination of traits. This classification becomes a prescription of what a human being is to be, to the extent that – in its own legal terms – it forges the human being herself, who becomes representative of all human beings, without any consideration of their actual differences. Nowadays, the classificatory outcomes of these strategies is reinforced by the common reliance on the language of rights, which, as I have demonstrated in Chapters 4 and 5, shapes the discourse in a very specific way.

Yet, the presence of similarities should not lead us to overlook the dissimilarities of inclusive strategies. The employment of a determinate legal language and the subsequent tendency towards a political lexicon characterized by a classificatory mark are integrated into dynamics that are distinctive and typical of each of them. To pin them down, it is of help to see how different types of policies translate into particular forms of governing. To this end, I will draw on a tripartition of governing techniques advanced by Davina Cooper (1998:11–14). In her analysis of the ways in which legal means structure a society's symbolic universe, Cooper identifies three modes of governing and examines their collateral (that is non-strictly political) productions and upshots. She elaborates on a model in which forms of governance are classified in accordance to criteria of visibility and capillarity. Based on this analysis, she draws up an ascending taxonomy that starts with the plainest and most transparent way of governing, "direct governance", and continues with increasingly articulated and opaque forms, which she calls "mid-way governance" and "governance at a distance".

Direct governance is a form of governing mostly based on a clear relationship between the state and social actors, and mainly organized around the straight imposition of authority by the former on the latter. The state exercises its power by setting out rules that channel and restrict people's discretion. Direct interventions are not limited to overt constraints or limitations, but often entail productive acts, such as the allocation of resources and the provisions of public services. Whether by creating a welfare system, conferring a right, or banning a practice, this form of governance appears as extremely transparent: all of its parts are traceable, from the source of authority (the state), to its productions (which takes the form of tangible, public and debated laws), up to the targets of its interventions (usually specified in legal texts, but in any case, defined and specified). In short, direct governance constitutes a straightforward relational form of subjection in which the two poles involved are linked by a cluster of public, explicit norms, which are produced by one pole and are meant to be acquired by, and complied with, the other. In this case, outcomes that exceed political rationality, producing ambiguous and unexpected interactions (which go beyond a "one-to-one" direct pattern – e.g. order-conformity, noncompliance-sanction) somewhat represent a degeneration of this process of governing.

Opportunity-oriented policies fit the model of direct government. This can be seen both in the case of enfranchisement and the discussion of the public/private divide. For what concerns enfranchisement, it is possible to describe this inclusive measure as a very direct way of promoting participation of all citizens in "public life". In fact, targets, recipients and results of legal measures are clear, explicit and transparent. Even the attainment of this aim appears, in the eyes of the law, as a plain process, which comes to be fulfilled in the mere affirmation of the legal decision itself. Enfranchisement, as well as the other policies promoted by opportunity-oriented strategies, can be characterized as the opening up of empowering positions. In this sense, the law fulfils its purposes simply by making accessible tools for one to exercise one's own political agency. In the allocation of equal and widespread public entitlements, opportunity-oriented policies perform their major political task; the control over the actual effects exerted on social actors and social bodies would exceed it.

It would be a mistake, though, to conclude that the lack of interest for their indirect results displayed by opportunity-oriented policies, entails the absence of such results. This crystal-clear pattern of direct governing, in fact, is also replete with scarcely visible relapses. An instance of this might be seen in those situations where opportunity-oriented policies are issued without considering the consequences exerted on the "private" sphere. Another example is the regulation of prostitution. Consider the failure of two opposite ways of dealing with this issue: decriminalization and legalization, specifically as enacted respectively in Sweden and Germany. In both cases, interventions mirror the model of direct governance: their purposes are as clear as the social bodies they address and the means they adopt. However, there is more than meets the eye, as indicated by the protests of sex workers and by rates of violence and exploitation. The criminalization of the client as well as the creation of "safer" spaces for sex workers, typical of decriminalizing strategies, do not impact on clusters of physical and symbolic violence, let alone on submerged exploitation, which is reproduced in cloistered sites and sites that are not reached by the law (as it were, in the private sphere). Abortion laws lend themselves as a further glaring example. Without looking at specific cases, it is generally true that abortion laws are structured around this form of governing, since they function exactly either through prohibition or through provisions about, and coercive limits on, personal agency. Once more, these regulations are clear, top-down and publicly accessible in all their parts, but do not take into account what falls outside the purview of the law. Illegal abortion procedures and practices of "home-abortion" are not considered into legal texts but constitute a predictable corollary of laws deriving from the strict enforcement of direct imperatives.[1]

The reason why I placed emphasis on undesired and unexpected "side effects" of direct techniques of governing has to do with the fact that the other forms of governance ("mid-way" and "at a distance") also exert effects that are not immediately visible in the direct relation between the legal text and the section of reality it focuses on. Mid-way governance and governance at a distance entail an even subtler and more implicit exercise of political authority, which is no longer conveyed only by the issuing of laws but is channelled by the instantiation of discursive devices.

In governing at a distance, the organization and management of norms of conduct and bureaucratic procedures, specific expertise and clusters of extra-political rules turn into primary outcomes of governance, replacing the typical productions of governing institutions. The system that characterizes at-a-distance regimes exceeds the one-to-one relationship that structures direct governance, as it veils both the recipients and the issuers of the intricate web of controlling devices. Legal interventions appear to be two-sided, as the

1 Among the most recent publication on the outcomes of legal regulation on prostitution and abortion, see, respectively Wagenaar (2017) and Berer (2017), Jones et al. (2018).

"actual" law (that constitutes a form of direct governing) always embroils a discursive pattern to support itself. In this case, the reception of the letter of the law is not separable from the reception of its symbolic implications. Therefore, this governing technique no longer functions on the basis of a threat of sanction (that is, through punishment of a given set of external behaviors meant to discourage them), but rather tends to be adopted as a reason for action beyond any legal obligation. In other words, the symbolic assumptions underlying the law tends to be internalized by social actors, so as to steer their actions and guide them. Such a process of incorporation alters the relationship established between governing institutions and social actors, as it turns from a transparent one to a complex tangle of legal and non-strictly legal devices, with which individuals have to deal. In this framework, the figure of the addressee of the law stands out as a more definite (although often more general) one, while both its contents and its source fade away. As a result, governing at a distance denotes a situation of poor visibility and high capillarity. In sum, governing at a distance is a way of

> guiding the actions of subjects through [...] normative inculcation so that they govern themselves [...] in the sense that they 'know' [...] what is appropriate and inappropriate behaviour. [...] A key quality of governing at a distance is that it appears impersonal and anonymous. The rules established are both general in character and do not appear to originate anywhere in particular. [...] [The] existence [of such codes of conducts] is rarely apparent. (Cooper 1998:12)

While direct governing externally compels individuals to do or to avoid certain actions and governing at a distance impacts on their activities by promoting internalization, mid-way governing promotes a technique that lies in between the other two. In this last form of governing, legal interventions shape and organize specific social entities as politically relevant in order to treat them as natural entities which have entered the political space because of their (political) relevance. Legal measures and techniques insulate (claimed) natural, pre-existing objects and redefine them in political terms. In this sense, mid-way governing shares aspects with both the other two forms. While direct governing hinges on an image of society as an artificial political construction whose legal traces are plainly visible and while governing at a distance posits the existence of a natural, self-regulating society and thus conceals its direct political intervention, mid-way governing has a bifid nature. This hampers a full internalization of the values and principles mid-way governing conveys, since the possibility of tracking down the origin of laws and their implications to a somehow tangible body leads social actors to follow – rather than embrace – norms in conformity with their goals. It is not uncommon for social actors to see "mid-way regulations" as strategies or tactics, that is, as something that institutionalizes non-political entities and that can be used in order to obtain personal achievements. Mid-way governing provides a stronger form of control than the mere regulation of external actions, since even if subjects perceive the cultural contours of the legal tools that are at their disposal, they never really get to reckon with the political and symbolical background of the contents that underpin these legal tools. In short, mid-way governing might be seen as a technique based on an "anamorphic visibility" – where governing devices seem transparent as in direct governance, but in reality, promote ideological assumptions as in governing at a distance –, with a (concealed) high degree of capillarity, as actors might perceive their relation to legal tools as strategic, but at the same time be unaware of the range of naturalized assumptions they are accepting.

While I associated opportunity-oriented policies with direct governance, capability-based and category-protecting policies can be regarded as instances of mid-way and at-a-distance techniques. Both capability-based and category-protecting policies, in fact, convey a set of (unstated) presuppositions through the enactment of specific and apparently clear-cut measures. Such premises might go from the delineation of a (one and only one) human form of living to the naturalization and essentialization of some identity features. Moreover, both cases require the compliance of their addressees, as well as their tacit acceptance of the presuppositions instantiated in the law. This "total agreement" fosters simultaneously the inclusion of the legal grammar in the broader framework of subjects' everyday reality, and the constitution of a legal platform, which is seemingly negotiable by single actors.

Mid-way governance and governance at a distance cast light on the two-sided character of legal measures. Throughout this work, I claimed that unsuccessful consequences of inclusive strategies demonstrate that legal regulations play an exceeding role in rapport to their "proper" domain. Due to their extra-legal effects, these forms of government finally appear to hold considerable symbolic power over everyday lives of social actors. This has been made clear by the discussion of how the jargon of rights affects social classifications and individual recognition, as well as the very possibility of one's giving an account of one's own identity. Laws, rulings and legal instances actively operate in the formulation of political conflicts and public debates. Such an activity cannot be reduced to the settlement of disputes, but results in a meta-articulation, that is, in the production of a narration based on the legal articulation of the case. This "specialized tale" about everyday life comes to intersect the way in which ordinary situations are verbalized. Law transcends the crafting and managing of isolated legal categories (the citizen, the human being, the homosexual) and engages in forms of meta-governance that affects the very possibility of the legal discourse itself and of the social perception of some signifiers. In other words, law obtains the status of a "structural discursive device" (see Cooper 1998), which organizes the domain of the possible and thus shapes the broader domain of the intelligible.

"Possibility" and "intelligibility" might be seen as two stages of a process of sociopolitical recognition, in which the former is the "proper" moment of legal recognition (the legal ratification of a status and its subsequent inclusion in the domain of socio-legal possibilities), while the latter is the horizon, also shaped by the law, beyond which entities are not (and cannot be) cognizable. My claim is that the way in which a governing body gives relevance to a social entity affects the structural opportunity for such an entity to enter the domain of speakability, finding a place in a symbolic field structured by the law. In a moment of increasing juridification, where peer-to-peer relationships and "transactions" are increasingly proceduralized (see West 2011), social recognition is often contingent on such a legal legitimation. While the social context appears to be at the same time rarefied and hypertrophic, legal recognition plays a major role in the emergence of socially ratified realities. These come to be highlighted and chosen among the plethora of different forms of life so as to become identifiable as discrete, sharp entities. Needless to say, the legal recognition to which I refer is no longer to be understood as a mere process of institutionalization; instead, it constitutes the excessive moment of the law, one in which politics and language interact to produce symbolic meanings.

My contention is that the process of human kinds production, on which all policies rely on, and the types of governing techniques that they incorporate, make sense of the deep-rooted connection between speakability and legal recognition. Let me expand on this aspect to claim that this relation is shaped by a specific way of governing that is primarily exerted on language, which in turn impacts remarkably on the symbolic resources underlying legal recognition.

Indications, guidelines, recommendations, standards and parameters provided in and through the law impact on the social realm, particularly as they delineate the possibility for groups (in their being representatives of human kinds) to be recognized in the social field – a delineation that also operates as a meta-delineation establishing what the (material and symbolic) conditions for the determination of these possibilities are, which I call intelligibility. Within the framework of this double dynamic, "possibility" and "intelligibility" mark out the spaces in which legal recognition can actually take place. Following Cooper (1998:17), we can define this double dynamic as "governance of governance", in which law

> can operate [on the governing process] through constraint, such as the judicial imposition of additional criteria to restrict and skew political discretion [...] [or can] work by redefining the identity of subordinate governance bodies [...] [and the] power relations between governing bodies.

This form of governance is a key hallmark of today's new composition of law and politics insofar as legal measures operate reflexively on the space of action of governing institutions by tracing the borders of legitimate intervention. This entails the designation of a system in which only a finite number of models, forms and procedures of recognition are made available, and where it is much more difficult than in other models of governance to perceive, indicate and recognize all that does not fit the resulting schema of intelligibility. Therefore, governance of governance implicitly (that is, with no direct provisions or visible constraints) provides a basic format for legal recognition. It is in this way that governance of governance affects how "debates are held – organising certain issues in, whilst others are organised out" (Cooper 1998:17).

The previous chapters of this book (Chapters 5 and 6) offered a few insights into the nested processes of preclusion and exclusion, acceptance and allowance that are sparked off through both an institutional linguistic operation and an operation on the language of institutions. On the one hand, the systematization of potential forms and contents of legal productions is inseparable from a validation of legitimate modalities and legitimate "proxies" or mediators. On the other hand, the very legitimation (here we are moving to a meta-meta-level) authorizes a speech that cannot but state what it is doomed to state, in the way it must be stated. As I showed in particular with regard to category-protecting policies (although, as I mentioned above, this applies also to other models), the legitimation of speech proceeds along the line of the legal identification of certain groups, to which representation is offered as long as they conform to given parameters. Interestingly, the primary outcome of this loop is that what gets legitimated as authorized speech reflects something that is already visible, socially recognized (indeed, it is not possible to authorize a non-recognizable entity) and, hence, represented speech is the bearer of a former recognition.

Based on these considerations, I would like to argue that policies aimed at promoting inclusion appear, first and foremost, like an a-critic ratification of an extant symbolic system. By way of a governance of governance, inclusive policies are doomed to fail to genuinely accommodate difference, as they devise ways for tackling marginalization through the pursuit of an assimilationist project. For, they all allow their addressees to articulate different and variegated situations with reference to a unifying scheme. This way of filtering political instances has an effect on the agency of social actors, since it deploys a cognitive effect that shapes (or better, makes and unmakes, produces, destroys) the elements that inhabit the social realm.

While governance of governance is the reworking of the boundaries of the possibility for subjects to be heard (which is already conditional upon them being intelligible), their (often progressive) focus on inclusion conceals the cognitive and substantive limits imposed on social subjects themselves. In this way, people's use of the tools offered by these policies implies a recognition that is also a misrecognition. To say it with Pierre Bourdieu (1991:127), these policies require "a form of recognition of this order, the kind implied by the misrecognition of the arbitrariness of its foundations". On Bourdieu's view, the efficacy of people's account of themselves and their problematic situations (those accounts that have the potential to exert legal effects) resides in the relation that exists between these very accounts and the available scheme of filtration. As a consequence, the indirect constraints imposed on them can be described as a "labour of enunciation", which is

> necessary in order to externalize the inwardness, to name the unnamed and to give the beginnings of objectification to pre-verbal and pre-reflexive dispositions and ineffable and unobservable experiences, through words which by their nature make them common and communicable, therefore meaningful and socially sanctioned. It may also be accomplished [...] in the transgression which is indispensable in order to name the unnameable, to break the censorships, institutionalized or internalized, which prohibit the return of the repressed. (Bourdieu 1991:129)

The way in which legal classifications, implemented through governance of governance, objectify and make certain experiences visible might either comply with the available symbolic framework or move away from it. In the second case, however, experiences appear as a rupture, a transgression – as Bourdieu says, that breaks the silence of an unspeakable condition. The very emergence of nonconforming social realities sets off discursive processes meant to address unforeseen situations with a view of anticipating the changes they might produce in the existing symbolic framework. In this sense, since "law cannot always fully exclude the issues it perceives as insignificant" (Cooper 1998:18), governing bodies are engaged in a battle over social grammar, which takes place by the doing, redoing and undoing of human kinds. In a few words, the labour of enunciation performed by newly formed groups is scarcely conceivable as entirely subversive.

When it emerges as the rise of alternatives that exceed the boundaries of the existing symbolic framework, marginalization appears as a serious challenge: difficult to tackle politically, its complexity calls for compassion and at the same time, sparks alert. These two ways of addressing marginalization come to be recomposed in the rhetoric of inclusion. While bringing about a widespread tolerance towards nonconforming realities, inclusion triggers a normalizing discourse that bears significant effects both at the political and symbolic levels.

The outcomes of narrow inclusive formulas affect the actual life of discriminated groups by determining the conditions of their social experience as well as the conditions for verbalizing them. On the other hand, at a symbolic level, processes of marginalization and inclusion are subjected to the same linguistic making up: the very account of what marginalization is and who the "marginalized human kinds" are, is deeply connected with available accounts and practices. Similarly, attempts of inclusion work along the lines of recognition and legitimation that draw on a codified jargon. In pursuing such an aim, policies and legal reforms constantly refer to a semantic repertoire that allows them to frame unfamiliar situations by relying on already accepted meanings. This hampers the perception of alternative forms of living, which are displayed as always consistent with hegemonic standards. From women equality to disability-friendly accommodations, up to LGBT families and new kinship formations, the logic of the "in and out" cannot but follow assimilating procedures of normalization. Inclusive discourses draw on a language that reconfirms and reproduces a determinate (contingent and partial) matrix, which erases differences in the name of an indefinite extension of legal patterns of recognition.

The clash between a commitment to plurality and the necessary devotion to a cluster of sedimented meanings eventuates in the creation of policies that are intended to comply with differences by deploying (whether explicitly or implicitly) concepts of equality, sameness, identity.

To comply with ambiguous needs, policymakers are called to implement extremely flexible legal patterns, which allow for the accommodation of the broadest variety of social instances with the smallest effort (Edelman 2011; McRuer 2006). This mechanism supports fundamental and human rights, once they become devices that fit different purposes by providing a-specific tools capable of functioning in all kinds of situations and address single, simple, univocal elements of society. Subjects of rights (as the citizen and the human being or the bearer of a definite identity) are cleared from all their incidental prerogatives, so as to constitute a "minimal functional unit" for the law. The combination between the super-adaptability of legal tools and the oversimplification of the addressees of norms is at the basis of the vast acceptance gained by the jargon of rights. Still, it is also at the origin of the dissolution of more committed political battles. Flexibility weakens the commitments that marked the relationship among political actors and loosens reciprocal ties of responsibility. At the same time, flexibility furthers individualized actions, which facilitate personal engagement in the expression of one's own political demands, while favoring an image of subjects as isolable components of the social realm. On the part of the state, this trend promotes the implementation of policies that ratify the monadic status of social actors by addressing atomistic elements of society (whether these are single individuals or individuals grouped together in fixed groups), obscuring the several interrelations and combined side effects of political interventions (Crenshaw 1989).

The distinction among policy approaches I offered in this work was meant to cast light on the static nature of policies that do not challenge the premises that cause marginalization, offering ready-made solutions that always imply the embracement (and the deployment) of a central perspective (hooks 1984, 2000). In the light of the examination carried out so far, we can finally see that the negligence of inclusive policies does not reside in their distinctive respective pitfalls, as it rather lies in a sort of "original sin" that concerns them all. The theoretical model that supports current inclusive policies are based on the subtle implementation of governance of governance that steers institutions in such a way that they fail to challenge hegemonic positions and to corrode conservative forms of living. To put it roughly, inclusion becomes the yoke that tames nonconforming realities by means of a compassionate invitation to join normality. Common linguistic formulas and practices are extended to those who were excluded exactly from (and by) these very practices, so that inclusion proceeds not from the embracement of different, multiple, nonconforming instances, but from their revision in the name of pre-existent, already settled and accepted institutes (Swennen and Croce 2015). Such an extension does not entail the erasure of deviant realities, which come to be absorbed (rhetorically, "accepted") as "they are", since they are not asked to renounce to their superficial narrations, and certainly not to their usual habits, but only to adapt such narrations and habits to a specific matrix.

In the last pages of this work, I will make the case that the main way to tackle marginalization effectively is to work on the boundaries imposed by the governance of governance on the existing models of legal recognition. This does not imply that rebellious or even revolutionary policies are needed, given the scarce practicability of this solution in the existing sociopolitical conditions. However, if the stake is the speakability of condition of marginalized reality, I will contend that crucial symbolic resources can be drawn from narrower and less ambitious contexts where alternatives are concretely performed in daily life.

This work has so far argued for a notion of unspeakability as something that should not be conceived as a side effect of inclusive policies, but that inheres in them. The core thesis I tried to justify is that predominant models of inclusive politics tend to identify spaces of intervention and to deploy mechanisms for redeeming the marginalized situation of those who dwell in these spaces. But it is in the identification of these spaces – that is, in the way policies construct their object – that something gets forged and, because of that, something else gets overshadowed, overlooked, neglected or even silenced. Although not exhaustive of all-inclusive democratic politics, the three models that I focused on in the first part of this book elucidate how this materially occurs. Policies that are concerned with the redistribution of opportunities assume the existence of a citizen as a "blank slate", that is, a public citizen, stripped of her private conditions, who can participate in the public life of her polity when (public, political) conditions are provided. In doing so, it brackets away the deep-seated link between marginalization in the public and in the private spheres. In contrast, policies that adopt a capabilist approach acknowledge the relevance of the latter and claim it is people's everyday life and ordinary practices that are to be taken into account by the government. However, this admission comes at a price. This model postulates the existence of a human nature which pinpoints the formulation of a range of hierarchically ordered, pregiven, almost invariable traits defining the human. This cuts out other facets of everyday experience, which are ipso facto dehumanized, or rendered unsuitable to sociability. Finally, policies working with categories set in motion a particularly interesting connection between the production of means for knowing and interpreting the world (seemingly devoid of political bearings) and legal measures meant to grant recognition. Here the underpinning mechanisms of object construction are conspicuously laid bare: the law touches what it sees and sees what it names.

While my analysis does not advocate a wholesale dismissal of inclusive policies as such, my interest is theoretically-driven insofar as I concerned myself with what the subject is required to do in order to become visible, audible and speakable in the eyes of political and legal institutions. This is why, in the second part of this book, I focused on how social subjects get involved in the production of those categories that institutions use to lay out instruments for granting recognition. By doing so, I intended to bring out the different features of today's legal rights (the prime instrument to grant and obtain recognition) *vis-à-vis* more conventional understandings of legal measures. Present-day rights bespeak and entail, at least to some extent and with regional variations, the demise of politics as a shared project of reimagining a society. If legal rights have long been (with important limits and non-negligible exclusions) meant to serve as the precondition for political participation, nowadays they are the condition for political visibility. They are what makes a subject what she is, but often in stark opposition to a bloated and static political machinery, more and more blind to the needs and claims of its citizens. And yet, Chapter 6 showed, for citizens to make use of these potent legal instruments, they have to pre-adjust, or at least re-adjust, their language to a normalizing institutional discourse, which filters relevant inputs and draws a path for attaining recognition and the benefits attached to it. It is for these last pages to offer glimpses into what can be done to lessen the exclusionary effects of this new composition of the political and the legal spheres. I will first delineate two models of conducting political battles meant to bestow speakability on those life forms and conditions that are left unspoken by inclusive politics and then argue that heed should be paid to micropolitical contexts that are replete with symbolic potential, whether or not they represent practicable alternatives on a large scale.

A first, more conventional way to realign politics and law is a bold politics of re-politicization. This might take the shape of a far-reaching process of denaturalization of naturalizing processes and historicization of dehistoricizing dynamics (as Bourdieu [1991, 1998] would have it), carried out through orchestrated and vociferous public battles from below (but see also Butler 1990/1999, 1993, 1997a: Chapters 2–4). This model and its inborn contradictions are well exposed in the last pages of Bourdieu's (2001) *Masculine Domination*, where he takes up the problem of political categorization (although in a slightly different manner than I did following Ian Hacking) to understand how marginalized groups can undo marginalization in non-dominant ways. The French author has in mind a more traditional politic of boisterous claim-making that, on the one hand, rejects the institutional setting and, on the other, want to be heard by it. Bourdieu deftly identifies one of the main problems affecting groups' movement politics, to wit, the fact that the group, as I abundantly showed in other ways, must constitute itself as a group to wage this battle. The orchestrated side of this enterprise is that groups are imagined as able to overstep their limited concerns and to attune themselves to the concerns of other groups that live in a situation of marginalization, most often due to other causes. In this sense, the battle of groups would not be intended to obtain a narrow form of recognition in the shape of, for instance, marriage rights or religious exemptions. These battles are imagined as levelling a further-reaching critique against interlocked spheres of oppression that glue together marginalization and political invisibility. Again, the core of the battle would be the *prise de conscience* that political visibility has to be politically framed, that is, it has to challenge the structuration of the political sphere as a whole. And yet, to embark on such a demanding activity and to acquire political consciousness, the group has first to acquire the consciousness of being a group. Put otherwise, the group must configure itself as a group that makes claims as such. However, this group is constituted as a group within and through those dominant categories that the group has to challenge in order to challenge the political sphere as a whole. In short, the group has to make use of the category it wants to reject. In sketching this model, Bourdieu is not entirely clear, and his writing betrays some degrees of uncertainty about whether this project can really be pulled off. Indeed, he seems to assume that there is no alternative to such a *prise de conscience* and thus to the somewhat strategic use of the semantic grid that groups are confronted with. He views this as a major problem, and the solution he suggests is a critical scrutiny of this process being at work. In his words, the group should unceasingly carry out, as it were, a metalevel activity whereby the group objectivates its own political strategy that it deploys as a group. With reference to the male/female classificatory hierarchy, he writes:

> Only political action that really takes account of all the effects of domination that are exerted through the objective complicity between the structure embodied in both women and men and the structure of the major institutions through which not only the masculine order but the whole social order is enacted and reproduced [...] will be able, no doubt in the long term and with the aid of contradiction inherent in the various mechanism or institutions concerned, to contribute to the progressive withering away of masculine domination. (Bourdieu 2001:117)

In the context of present-day politics, I see this strategy as destined to fall through because of two main reasons, one historical and the other theoretical. First, the disjunction between politics and law has produced effects of fragmentation that are not simply dysfunctional to traditional politics but are functional to a much broader organization of law at a supra-state level. What is known as "legal globalization" is, at one and the same time, an effect and an active agent of the collapse of state-based legal systems. The way law works today is much less attuned to local values and needs and much less amenable to the intertranslatability of legal languages, whether or not anchored to a national state. Work on multiple processes of segmentation and private constitutionalization of these segments do a good job in showing that the inner logic of legal production is more and more disconnected from moments of local public deliberation (see e.g. Croce and Goldoni 2015; Goldoni 2014). Yet, this is not only dysfunctional: the law, as I illustrated mainly with reference to the jargon of rights, successfully produces effects that change people's lives, whether or not this happens in keeping with the conventional principles of the democratic co-constitution of law and politics. Law's being effective – and being effective in a way that maps onto the different fragments of society and their needs – is perhaps the main obstacle for this first solution. This is why I tried to portray the withdrawal of the state not as an accidental failure, but as a different mode of governing. This leads me to discuss the theoretical reason behind why a straightforward realignment of law and politics can hardly succeed.

The current mutual position of law to politics is instrumental in the production of a specific composition of society, where groups themselves contribute to the production of the categories through which they get recognized. The subject is by no means annihilated. Rather, she is thoroughly involved in the delineation of the semantic grid through which institutions name and view them. It is not coincidence that throughout this work I insisted on a mechanism of "feedback loop", where none of the parties is still and passive. The parties involved, albeit to different degrees (depending on the contextual situation), contribute to a joint activity of mutual recognition that can be performed precisely because this activity occurs in smaller institutional fragments than traditional democratic arenas (whether formal, such as parliaments, or more informal, such as civil society or the public sphere).

In the face of this likely failure, a second model to trigger a strategy of re-politicization is the enactment of alternative practices in micropolitical contexts. A shift occurs from a conceptual to a contextual re-politicization, where political action is focused

> on a range of tasks, from denaturalizing the status quo to stimulating and educating the imagination, promoting a desire for change, demonstrating the limits of what can be thought of, and performing textually and experimentally the political struggles that change invokes. (Cooper 2013:44)

On this view, such activities are carried out through the enactment of concrete alternative political scenarios, for, this second model actualizes ordinary social practices in unconventional ways, within restricted communities, in order to operate a re-articulation of the categories and concepts at play in mainstream political arrangements. Therefore, the term "contextual" invokes the strong relation that these political practices have with their context, in particular with the time(s) and the space(s) in which they come into being. The radical embeddedness of such enacted practices and, at the same time, their decided disjunction from mainstream realities have led scholars to identify contextual re-politicization with what is now known as "everyday utopias" (Cooper 2013; on "contemporary" utopia, see also Levitas 2007; Lewis and Neal 2005; Schönpflug 2008; Wegner 2002). Far from retaining its traditional, value-laden, ideal and perfectionist meaning (observable in the double characterization of utopia both as "ou-topia" and as "eu-topia" – respectively no-place and good place – see Schönpflug 2008:7), everyday utopias are (spatially and temporarily) accessible sites in which "counterintuitive ways" (Cooper 2013:27) of coping with ordinary situations are imagined, designed and practiced. Examples of everyday utopias are such communities in which common practices are performed in different and innovative ways, for instance – as Cooper (2013) indicates – LETS (Local Exchange Trading System) and trading groups that work with local currency or more generally without money (as in the case of time banking); schools built on methods and ideals of a democratic nature (such as Summerhill School in the UK or schools that adopt the Reggio Emilia Approach); or even some nudist performances.

The concreteness of the examples provided shows that everyday utopias do not shape up imaginary places of perfect politics, nor do they indicate a modality for leaving behind mainstream social interactions in order to enter a temporary space of ideality (Wegner 2002:17–39). Rather, they lay the foundations for a re-attunement to the political based on concrete daily interactions. The utopia of a better world is not the production of an all-encompassing, totalizing political project, but the shared performance of more viable and satisfying social dynamics. Re-politicization is carried out through collective practices that target very specific segments of people's lives (e.g. sexual intercourses, money, education, sociability) with the aim of producing a viable alternative to mainstream inflections of everyday situations. It is important to remark that none of these realities pursues change for its own sake, as at the core of such communities lies an interest in responding to prosaic, concrete, quotidian needs and difficulties by exploring other ways of coping with particular moment of everyday life. Therefore, the utopian element does not reside in the idyllic imagining of a better world in a fictional, fictitious dimension, but in the daily and micro-contextual actualization and re-elaboration of meanings, concepts and arrangements that are commonly taken for granted. Here, the taken-for-grantedness that silences marginalized subjects is interrogated and questioned, eventually overturned in the pursuit of alternative methods and approaches.

The reformulation that Utopian practices allows and encourages is not contingent on the mainstream scenario, since it opposes (most often indirectly) what exists through a critical engagement that does not neglect (or try to annihilate) it. The operation of displacement undertaken in these minor-stream contexts does eventuate neither in the creation of insulated counter-communities in which ordinary practices are distorted and reshaped in service of partial, particular projects or programs, nor in the reproduction of mainstream modalities, that is, in the arrangement of monolithic counter-communities that aim at substituting the "normal" one. Rather, everyday utopias are oriented towards destabilizing the apparently secure status quo of mainstream reality by imagining and enacting an immanent rethinking of existing social connections (such as sexual pleasure, trading, hierarchical structures, the relation with the environment and others). The fact that the actualization of "better" ways of living starts on a small-scale basis and is configured as a non-totalizing way of living (that is, the reduced space and the limited temporality of everyday utopias) constitutes the kernel of a polymorph, dynamic, re-articulation of the political. In effect, the fragmented nature of minor-stream groups and/or organizations, as well as their proximity (both physical, as they are not elsewhere, and practical, as they touch upon commonplace concerns) to mainstream institutions lead to the articulation of innovative practices which intersect and interact with traditional ones. Moreover, this articulation does not presuppose the mastery of a language that, as I extensively argued, risks falling prey to dominant signifiers and grids of meanings; rather it takes the concrete path of material interactions where new meanings are produced precisely in virtue of their potential conflict with dominant signifiers and grids of meanings. Because of this orthogonal relation to the mainstream, Cooper (2013:6) describes everyday utopias as “social black holes, absorbing those who enter but missing from prevailing maps of their field”. This label nicely displays the high pervasivity and permeability of these sites, in which “a focus on the everyday extends into utopia” and where “prosaic dimensions of regular life – sex, trading, teaching, politics, public appearance, and speech – are performed in innovative and socially ambitious ways that, by challenging, simultaneously unvail prevailing norms, ideologies, and practices” (Cooper 2004:6).

Portraying re-politicization as the collective actualization of alternative imaginaries spotlights the strong link among political concepts, symbolical structures and material arrangements. Everyday utopias become sites of political reformulation at the very moment in which they cease to be self-excluding manifestations of discomfort and begin to set in motion a series of “epistemologies of the margin” (Cooper 2013:32; see also hooks 1991). These are not only the expression of a critique of dominant ways of living, but are above all, the structuration of (physical, symbolic and political) sites where it is possible to experience “what other kinds of forms [of living] could be like” (Cooper 2013:32). The experience of these alternatives might be both active (as enacted and achievable) and passive (as witnessed and observable), since the openness of these sites not only allows participant to go to and fro, but also to become the mediators between such nonconforming practices and the mainstream context. In this sense, flexibility and proximity are two of the most important features of this second model of re-politicization.

On the one hand, the flexible variety of participants brings about an ever-changing oscillation between the moment of actualization and the moment of imagination of alternative good spaces. Participants’ differences in needs and desires, ideals and longings subject minor-stream communities to the continuous and incessant reformulation of the utopic imaginary (that – for this reason – are unlikely to turn into an ideology, in which a fixed status quo has to be sustained; see Levitas 2007) and, consequently, to a reassessment and re-evaluation of practices themselves. However, conflicts and failures to which these sites, because of their inherent uncertainty, are exposed should not be seen as pitfalls or flaws. The articulation of a desire for more livable contexts is actually contingent on the provisionality of these practices, for it is exactly by virtue of a dynamic articulation of premises and fundamental assumptions of the practice that the risk of dehistoricization and naturalization of the political and symbolic concepts produced can be avoided (see Levitas 2007).

On the other hand, proximity (or even promiscuity) of these sites and the mainstream social reality encourages to the reflexive game of comparison. The ostensive, though tentative, exhibition of alternatives paves the way for a renewed articulation of one's own situation. In this sense, the core of everyday utopias is not about dismantling or destabilizing the existing order, as they rather aspire to unsettle this order through the arrangement of non-competitive alternative forms of living. The non-totalizing tendency of these practices permits them to interact concretely with the hegemonic structure, without being forced to prove an ideal, inherent consistence. It is in their transience that everyday utopias fulfil a reinvigorating political task.

It is my claim that such a contextual re-politicization does not lapse back into the assimilatory dynamic that besets inclusive policies and threatens what I have called the "conceptual model". Everyday utopias might be taken as instances of political modalities to re-collocate symbolic resources at the margins. Thanks to their limitedness, they are able to challenge the hegemonic order without engaging in a dangerous tug of war against it. At the same time, their inherent variety and their ineffability contribute to make them sites of creation of a transformative politics:

> utopias emphasize the importance of transformed social existence to thinking differently. [...] It is not simply about the creation of worlds or ways of living that will better meet people's interests as they currently are. Utopia is also centrally concerned with those changing interests, desires, identifications, and forms of embodiment that happen as people (and other forms of life) experience other ways of living. (Cooper 2013:34)

Contextual re-politicization is not a recipe to the re-establishment of a thick state, nor is it the remedy to the mismatch between political procedures and legal techniques. The current state of affairs is such that social actors will predictably continue to seize on the rapid upsurge of legal rights as an effective, albeit normalizing, political tool. However, the opening up of microdynamics where people can experience the day-to-day organization of practices in subversive but ordinary ways (where subversion does not target "the system" as a whole, but the widespread understanding of how certain ordinary things have to be carried out) is likely to mine interstices where people can really regard themselves as "affected people", that is, people called upon to think up the alternative. In these interstices, the political gets back its original sense of reimagining the social and performatively affecting it, where imaginings and actualization can and often do diverge, but this divergence serves as a symbolic prism through which we can grasp reality's inevitable character of constructedness and artificiality, and thus, its amenability to revision. Contextual re-politicization, of which everyday utopias are an important example, is thus a small-scale but ambitious project (or dozens of micro-projects) where subjects, at least transitorily (not all their life, not all their time) become political subjects who get dirty hands to make decisions on how to do things in the here and now, who dare to be take responsibility for these decisions, who take the risk of making mistakes. In these contexts, rights and benefits are already and always political, because they display at once their face of choice, duty and responsibility; in these contexts, the marginal has always something to say the mainstream, and the unspeakable is systematically brought to bear on the speakable as the ever-present incongruity between what we hoped to achieve and what we failed to achieve.

Bibliography

Archibugi, D. & Beetham, D. (1998) *Diritti umani e democrazia cosmopolitica*, Milano: Feltrinelli.

Arfini, E. A. (2010) 'Istruzioni per diventare disabile. Un'analisi narrativa del progetto sul corpo transabile', in *Studi culturali*, 3: 343–364.

Arfini, E. A. (2014) 'Transability', in *TSQ: Transgender Studies Quarterly*, 1(1–2): 228–230.

Ayala Lopez, S. (2016) 'Speech Affordances: A Structural Take on How Much We Can Do With Our Words', in *European Journal of Philosophy*, 24(4): 879–891.

Barron, K. (2001) 'Autonomy in Everyday Life, for Whom?', in *Disability & Society*, 16(3): 431–447.

Bauman, Z. (1996) 'From Pilgrims to Tourists – Or a Short History of Identity', in Hall, S. & Du Gay, P. (eds.), *Question of Cultural Identities*, London: Thousand Oaks, pp. 18–36.

Bauman, Z. (2004) *Wasted Lives: Modernity and Its Outcasts*, Cambridge: Polity.

Bellamy, R. (2008) *Citizenship: A Very Short Introduction*, Oxford and New York: Oxford University Press.

Belmonti, M. G. et al. (1980) *Un processo per stupro*, Torino: Einaudi.

Benhabib, S. (1999) 'Sexual Difference and Collective Identities: The New Global Constellation', in *Signs*, 24(2): 335–361.

Berer, M. (2017) 'Abortion Law and Policy around the World: In Search of Decriminalization', in *Health and Human Rights*, 19(1): 13–27.

Bernini, L. (2013) *Apocalissi queer: Elementi di teoria antisociale*, Pisa: ETS.

Bernstein, M. (1997) 'Celebration and Suppression: The Strategic Uses of Identity by the Lesbian and Gay Movement', in *American Journal of Sociology*, 103(3): 531–565.

Berubé, M. (1996) *Life as We Know it: A Father, a Family, and an Exceptional Child*, New York: Pantheon Books.

Blackledge, A. (2005) *Discourse and Power in a Multilingual World*, Amsterdam: John Benjamins Publishing.

Bleier, R. (1984) *Science and Gender: A Critique of Biology and its Themes on Women*, New York: Pergamon.

Boesveld, S. (2015) 'Becoming Disabled by Choice, Not Chance: 'Transabled' People Feel Like Impostors in Their Fully Working Bodies', in *National Post*, 3 June, available on-line at http://news.nationalpost.com/news/canada/becoming-disabled-by-choice-not-chance-transabled-people-feel-like-impostors-in-their-fully-working-bodies (last accessed November 2018).

Borghi, R. (2012) 'Postporno. Questo porno che non è un porno', in Mascat, J. et al. (eds.), *Femministe a parole. Grovigli da districare*, Roma: Ediesse, pp. 219–225.

Botti, C. (2012), *Prospettive Femministe. Morale, bioetica e vita quotidiana*, Torino: Espress Edizioni.

Botti, C. (ed.) (2013) *Le etiche della diversità culturale*, Firenze: Le Lettere.

Bourdieu, P. (1991) *Language and Symbolic Power*, Cambridge: Polity Press.

Bourdieu, P. (1998) *Practical Reasons: On the Theory of Action*, Stanford (CA): Stanford University Press.

Bourdieu, P. (2001) *Masculine Domination*, Stanford (CA): Stanford University Press.

Bourdieu, P. (2004) 'The Mystery of Ministry: From Particular Wills to the General Will', in *Constellation*, 11(1): 37–43.

Braidotti, R. (1994) *Nomadic Subjects. Embodiment and Sexual Difference in Contemporary Feminist Theory*, New York: Columbia University Press.

Braidotti, R. (2003) 'Becoming Woman: Or Sexual Difference Revisited', in *Theory, Culture & Society*, 20(3): 43–64.

Braidotti, R. (2013) *The Posthuman*, Cambridge: Polity Press.

Brown, W. (1989) 'Book in Review: 'Feminism Unmodified'', in *Political Theory*, 17(3): 489–492.

Brown, W. (2000) 'Suffering Rights as Paradoxes', *Constellation*, 7(2): 230–242.

Brown, W. & Halley, J. E. (eds.) (2002) *Left Legalism/Left Critique*, Durham (NC) and London: Duke University Press.

Bufacchi, V. (2012) *Social Injustice. Essays in Political Philosophy*, London: Palgrave MacMillan.

Burke, L. et al. (eds.) (2000) *The Routledge Language and Cultural Theory Reader*, London: Routledge.

Butler, J. (1989) 'Foucault and the Paradox of Bodily Inscriptions', in *Journal of Philosophy*, LXXXVI(11): 601–607.

Butler, J. (1990/1999) *Gender Trouble. Feminism and the Subversion of Identity*, London and New York: Routledge.

Butler, J. (1993) *Bodies That Matter. On the Discursive Limits of 'Sex'*, London and New York: Routledge.

Butler, J. (1997a) *The Psychic Life of Power. Theories in Subjection*, Stanford (CA): Stanford University Press.

Butler, J. (1997b) *Excitable Speech: A Politics of the Performative*, London and New York: Routledge.

Butler, J. (1997c) 'Sovereign Performatives in the Contemporary Scene of Utterance', in *Critical Inquiry*, 23(2): 350–377.

Butler, J. (1997d) 'Merely Cultural', in *Social Text*, 52/53: 265–277.

Butler, J. (2000) *Antigone's Claim: Kinship between Life & Death*, New York: Columbia University Press.

Butler, J. (2004a) *Undoing Gender*, London and New York: Routledge.

Butler, J. (2005) *Giving an Account of Oneself*, New York: Fordham University Press.

Butler, J. & Athanasiou, A. (2013) *Dispossession: The Performative in the Political*, Cambridge: Polity Press.

Butler, J. & Spivak, G. C. (2007) *Who Sings the Nation-State? Language, Politics, Belonging*, Kolkata: Seagull book.

Butler, J. & Venditti, V. (2014) 'Reframing the Normal, Diffracting The Norm. An Interview with Judith Butler', *Politica & Società*, 3: 393–404.

Cady Stanton, E., Mott, L. et al. (1848) *The Declaration of Sentiments, Seneca Falls Conference*, available on-line at http://www.fordham.edu/halsall/mod/senecafalls.asp (last accessed November 2018).

Califia, P. (2003) *Ex Changes: The Politics of Transgenderism*, Berkeley (CA): Cleis Press.

Castells, M. (1972) *La Question urbaine*, Paris: Maspero.

Cavarero, A. (1997) *Tu che mi guardi, tu che mi racconti*, Roma: Feltrinelli.

Cavarero, A. (2014) *Inclinazioni. Critica alla rettitudine*, Milano: Raffaello Cortina Editore.

Cavarero, A. & Restaino, F. (2002) *Le filosofie femministe*, Milano: Bruno Mondadori.

Chasin, A. (2001) *Selling Out: The Gay and Lesbian Movement Goes to Market*, London: Palgrave Macmillan.

Cobb, M. (2011) 'Lonely', in Halley, J. E. & Parker, A. (eds.), *After Sex: On Writing Since Queer Theory*, Durham (NC) and London: Duke University Press, pp. 207–220.

Coccia, E. (2014) *Il bene nelle cose. La pubblicità come discorso morale*, Bologna: il Mulino.

Cooper, D. (1998) *Governing Out of Orders. Space, Law and the Politics of Belonging*, London: Rivers Oram Press.

Cooper, D. (2004) *Challenging Diversity. Rethinking Equality and the Value of Difference*, Cambridge: Cambridge University Press.

Cooper, D. (2013) *Everyday Utopias: The Conceptual Life of Promising Spaces*, Durham (NC): Duke University Press.

Corradetti, C. (ed.) (2012) *Philosophical Dimensions of Human Rights: Some Contemporary Views*, Dordrecht: Springer.

Cremonesi, V. (2012) 'Città e potere. Lo spazio urbano come organizzazione biopolitica', in *Materiali Foucaultiani*, 1(1): 91–110.

Crenshaw, K. (1989) 'Demarginalizing the Intersection of Race and Sex: A Black Feminist Critique of Antidiscrimination Doctrine, Feminist Theory and Antiracist Politics', in *The University of Chicago Legal Forum*, 1: 139–167.

Crispin, J. (2017) *Why I Am Not a Feminist*, Brooklyn and New York: Melville House.

Croce, M. (2015a) 'Homonormative Dynamics and the Subversion of Culture', in *European Journal of Social Theory*, 18(1): 3–20.

Croce, M. (2015b) 'Secularization, Legal Pluralism, and the Question of Relationship-Recognition Regimes', in *The European Legacy: Toward New Paradigms*, 20(2): 151–165.

Croce, M. (2015c) 'From Gay Liberation to Marriage Equality: A Political Lesson to be Learnt', in *European Journal of Political Theory*, 17(3): 280–299.

Croce, M. (2018) *Politics of Juridification*, London: Routledge.

Croce, M. & Goldoni, M. (2015) 'A Sense of Self-suspicion: Global Legal Pluralism and the Claim to Legal Authority', in *Ethics & Global Politics*, 8(1): 1–20.

Croce, M. & Salvatore, A. (2015) *Undoing Ties. Political Philosophy at the Waning of the State*, London: Bloomsbury.

Cutas, D. & Bortolotti, L. (2010) 'Natural versus Assisted Reproduction: In Search of Fairness', in *Studies in Ethics, Law, and Technology*, 4(1): 1–20.

Davidson, A.I. (2001) *The Emergence of Sexuality. Historical Epistemology and the Formation of Concepts*, Cambridge (MA): Harvard University Press.

Deleuze, G. (2004) *Desert Islands and Other Texts. 1953–1974*, Cambridge (MA) and London: Semiotext(e).

Deleuze, G. & Guattari, F. (1987) *A Thousand Plateaus: Capitalism and Schizofrenia*, Minneapolis: University of Minnesota Press.

Denbow, J. M. (2014) 'Reproductive Autonomy, Counter-conduct, and the Juridical', in *Constellation*, 21(3): 415–424.

Donlan, S. P. (2015) 'To Hibridity and Beyond: Reflections on Legal and Normative Complexity', in Palmer, V. V. et al. (eds.) *Mixed Legal Systems, East and West: Newest Trends and Developments*, Farnham: Ashgate, pp. 17–32.

Douglas, M. (1987) *How Institutions Think*, London: Routledge & Kegan Paul.

Duggan, L. (2003) *The Twilight of Equality? Neoliberalism, Cultural Politics, and the Attack on Democracy*, Boston: Beacon Press.

Edelman, L. (2011) 'Ever After: History, Negativity and the Social', in Halley, J. E. & Parker, A. (eds.), *After Sex: On Writing since Queer Theory*, Durham (NC) and London: Duke University Press, pp. 110–119.

Fassin, É. (2003) 'L'inversion de la question homosexuelle', in *Revue française de psychanalyse*, 67(1): 263–284.

Fausto-Sterling, A. (1993) 'The Five Sexes: Why Male and Female Are Not Enough', *The Science*, 33(2): 20–24.

Fausto-Sterling, A. (2012) 'The Dynamic Development of Gender Variability', *Journal of Homosexuality*, 59(3): 398–421.

Felman, S. (2002) *The Scandal of the Speaking Body, Don Juan with J.L. Austin or Seduction in Two Languages*, Stanford (CA): Stanford University Press.

Finnis, J. (2011) *Natural Law and Natural Rights*, 2nd ed., Oxford: Oxford University Press.

Formosa, P. & Mackenzie, C. (2014) 'Nussbaum, Kant, and the Capabilities Approach to Dignity', in *Ethical Theory and Moral Practice*, 17(5): 875–892.

Foucault, M. (2002) *The Order of Things. An Archaeology of the Human Sciences*, London and New York: Routledge

Franklin, S. (1997) *Embodied Progress: A Cultural Account of Assisted Conception*, London and New York: Routledge.

Freedman, E. (2002) *No Turning Back: The History of Feminism and the Future of Women*, London: Penguin.

Fricker, M. (2006) 'Powerlessness and Social Interpretation', in *Episteme*, 33(1–2): 96–108.

Friedan, B. (1963) *The Feminine Mystique*, New York: Norton.

Gamson, J. (1995) 'Must Identity Movements Self-destruct? A Queer Dilemma', in *Social Problems*, 42(3): 390–407.

Giglioli, D. (2014) *Critica della vittima. Un esperimento con l'etica*, Roma: Nottetempo edizioni.

Gilden, A. (2008) 'Toward a More Transformative Approach: The Limits of Transgender Formal Equality', in *Berkeley Journal of Gender, Law & Justice*, 23: 83–117.

Goffman, E. (1963) *Stigma*, London: Penguin.

Goldoni, M. (2014) 'The Politics of Global Legal Pluralism', in *Jura Gentium*, available on-line at doi:10.2139/ssrn.2448313 (last accessed October 2018).

Goode, E. (2013) 'Victims Push Laws to End Online Revenge Posts', in *The New York Times*, 24th September 2013, available on-line at http://www.nytimes.com/2013/09/24/us/victims-push-laws-to-end-online-revenge-posts.html?pagewanted=all&_r=0 (last accessed October 2018).

Grossi, P. (2005) *Il diritto tra potere e ordinamento*, Napoli: ESI.

Grossi, P. (2015), *Ritorno al diritto*, Roma & Bari: Laterza.

Guaraldo, O. (2015) 'Sul materno: ripensarne il senso tra biopolitica e femminismo', in Bernardini, M.G. & Orsetta Giolo, O. (eds.), *Critiche di genere. Percorsi su norme, corpi e identità nel pensiero femminista*, Roma: Aracne.

Habermas, J. (2005) *Die intersubjektive Verfassung des normengeleiteten Geistes, in Zwischen Naturalismus und Religion Philosophische Aufsätze*, Frankfurt am Main: Suhrkamp Verlag.

Hacking, I. (1986) 'Making up People', in Biagioli, M. (ed.), *The Science Studies Reader*, New York: Psychology Press, pp. 161–172.

Hacking, I. (1995a) 'The Looping Effect on Human Kinds', in Sperber, D. & Premack, D. (eds.), *Causal Cognition: A Multidisciplinary Debate*, Cambridge (MA): Harvard University Press, pp. 351–383.

Hacking, I. (1995b) *Rewriting the Soul: Multiple Personality and the Sciences of Memory*, Princeton (NJ): Princeton University Press.

Hacking, I. (1999) *The Social Construction of What?*, Cambridge (MA): Harvard University Press.

Halley, J. E. (2000) 'Like-Race Argument', in Butler, J. et al. (eds.), *What's Left of Theory? New Work on the Politics of Literary Theory*, London and New York: Routledge, pp. 40–74.

Halley, J. E. (2001) 'Recognition, Rights, Regulation, Normalization: Rhetorics of Justification in the Same-Sex Marriage Debate', in Wintemute, R. et al. (eds.), *Legal Recognition of Same-Sex Partnerships: A Study of National, European, and International Law*, London: Bloomsbury, pp. 97–109.

Halley, J. E. (2010) 'Behind the Law of Marriage (I): From Status/Contract to the Marriage System', in *Unbound*, 6(1): 1–58.

Haraway, D. (1981) 'In the Beginning Was the Word: The Genesis of Biological Theory', in *Signs*, 6(3): 469–481.

Haslanger, S. (2000) 'Gender and Race: (What) Are They? (What) Do We Want Them To Be?', in *Noûs*, 34(1): 31–55.

Haslanger, S. (2006) 'What Good Are Our Intuitions? Philosophical Analysis and Social Kinds', in *Aristotelian Society*, 80(1): 89–118.

Haslanger, S. (2012) *Resisting Reality: Social Construction and Social Critique*, New York: Oxford University Press.

Haslanger, S. (2015) 'The Normal, the Natural and the Good: Generics and Ideology', in *Politica & Società*, 3(1): 365–392.

Holmes, S. & Sunstein, C. R. (1999) *The Cost of Rights. Why Liberty Depends on Taxes*, New York: W.W. Norton & Company.

hooks, b. (1984) *Feminist Theory: From Margin to Center*, Boston: South End Press.

hooks, b. (1991) *Yearning: Race, Gender, and Cultural Politics*, London: Turnaround.

hooks, b. (1992) *Black Looks. Race and representation*, Boston (MA): South End Press.

hooks, b. (1994) *Teaching to Transgress. Education as the Practice of Freedom*, New York and London: Routledge.

hooks, b. (2000) *Feminism is for Everybody: Passionate Politics*, London: Pluto Press.

Howe, N. & Strauss, W. (2000) *Millennials Rising: The Next Great Generation*, London: Vintage Books.

Hyder, E. & Tissot, C. (2013) '"That's Definite Discrimination': Practice under the Umbrella of Inclusion', in *Disability & Society*, 28(1): 1–13.

Imrie, R. (2000) 'Disabling Environments and the Geography of Access Policies and Practices', in *Disability and Society*, 15(1): 5–24.

Jay, K. & Young, A. (1992) *Out of the Closet: Voices of Gay Liberation*, New York: New York University Press.

Jones, B. S. et al. (2018) 'State Law Approaches to Facility Regulation of Abortion and Other Office Interventions', in *American Journal of Public Health*, 108(4): 486–492.

Kafer, A. (2013) *Feminist Queer Crip*, Bloomington: Indiana University Press.

Kainz, H. P. (2004) *Natural Law: An Introduction and Re-Examination*, Chicago and La Salle (IL): Open Court.

Keller, E. F. (1995) *Reflections on Gender and Science*, New Haven: Yale University Press.

Kennedy, D. (2002) 'The Critique of Rights n Critical Legal Studies', in Brown, W. & Halley, J. E. (eds.), *Left Legalism/Left Critique*, Durham (NC) and London: Duke University Press, pp. 178–228.

Kumari Campbell, F. (2013) 'Re-cognising Disability: Cross-Examining Social Inclusion through the Prism of Queer Anty-sociality', in *Jindal Global Law Review*, 4(2): 209–239.

Lacey, N. (1997) 'Unspeakable Subjects, Impossible Rights: Sexuality, Integrity and Criminal Law', in *Women: A Cultural Review*, 8(2): 143–157.

Lacey, N. (1998) *Unspeakable Subjects. Feminist Essay in Legal and Social Theory*, Oxford: Hart Publishing.

Langton, R. (1993) 'Speech Acts and Unspeakable Acts', in *Philosophy & Public Affairs*, 22(4): 293–330.

Leckey, R. (2011a) 'Lesbian Parental Projects in Word and Deed', in *Revue Juridique Thémis*, 45: 315–341.

Leckey, R. (2011b) 'Law Reform, Lesbian Parenting, and the Reflective Claim', in *Social & Legal Studies*, 20: 331–348.

Lettieri, T. (2013) 'Disability Studies: spazio, accessibilità e diritti umani', in *Italian Journal of Disability Studies/Rivista Italiana di Studi sulla Disabilità*, 1(1): 133–150.

Levitas, R. (2007) 'Looking for the Blue: The Necessity of Utopia', in *Journal of Political Ideologies*, 12(3): 289–306.

Lewis, G. & Neal, S. (2005) 'Introduction: Contemporary Political Contexts, Changing Terrains and Revisited Discourses', in *Ethnic and Racial Studies*, 28(3): 423–444.

Livia, A. et al. (eds.) (1997) *Queerly Phrased. Language, Gender, and Sexuality*, Oxford: Oxford University Press.

Lloyd, M. (2007) *Judith Butler: From Norms to Politics*, Cambridge and Malden: Polity Press.

Lonzi, C. (2010) *Sputiamo su Hegel. E altri scritti*, Milano: et al.

MacKinnon, C. (1987) *Feminism Unmodified: Discourses on Life and Law*, Cambridge (MA) and London: Harvard University Press.

MacKinnon, C. (1989) *Toward a Feminist Theory of the State*, Cambridge (MA) and London: Harvard University Press.

MacKinnon, C. (1993) *Only Words*, Cambridge (MA) and London: Harvard University Press.

MacKinnon, C. (2006) *Are Women Human? And Other International Dialogues*, Cambridge (MA) and London: Harvard University Press.

Marzocchi, V. (2004) *Le ragioni dei diritti umani*, Napoli: Liguori.

Marzocchi, V. (2011) *Filosofia politica. Storia, concetti, contesti*, Roma-Bari: Laterza.

Marzocchi, V. (2014) 'What Can We Mean by Legal Pluralism? A Socio-philosophical Perspective', in *Jura Gentium*, available on-line at http://www.juragentium.org/Centro_Jura_Gentium/la_Rivista_files/JG_pluralismo.pdf (last accessed October 2018).

McConnel-Ginet, S. (2003) "What's in a name?' Social Labeling and Gender Practices', in Holmes, J. & Meyerhoff, M. (eds.), *The Handbook of Gender and Language*, Malden (MA): Blackwell, pp. 69–97.

McRuer, R. (2006) *Crip Theory. Cultural Signs of Queerness and Disability*, London and New York: New York University Press.

Medeghini, R. (2013) 'I diritti nella prospettiva dell'inclusione e dello spazio comune', in *Italian Journal of Disability Studies/Rivista Italiana di Studi sulla Disabilità*, 1(1): 93–108.

Menski, W. (2014) 'The Liquidity of Law as a Challenge to Global Theorising', in *Jura Gentium*, available on-line at http://www.juragentium.org/Centro_Jura_Gentium/la_Rivista_files/JG_pluralismo.pdf (last accessed September 2018).

Merry, S. E. (2006) 'Anthropology and International Law', in *Annual Review of Anthropology*, 35: 99–116.

Merry, S. E. (2008) 'International Law and Socio-legal Scholarship: Toward a Spatial Global Legal Pluralism', in *Studies in Law, Politics, and Society*, 41: 149–168.

Mitchell, D. T. (1999) 'Forewords', in Stiker, R. (ed.), *History of Disability*, Ann Arbor (MI): The University of Michigan Press.

Moati, R. (2014) *Derrida/Searle: Deconstruction and Ordinary Language*, New York: Columbia University Press.

Monceri, F. (2011) *Oltre l'identità sessuale. Teorie queer e corpi transgender*, Pisa: Edizioni ETS.

Monceri, F. (2012) 'Citizenship on Trial: 'Disability' and the Borders of Gender', in *AG AboutGender*, 1(2): 51–72.

Moyn, S. (2010) *The Last Utopia: Human Rights in History*, Cambridge (MA) and London: Harvard University Press.

Moyn, S. (2012) 'Do Human Rights Treaties Make Enough of a Difference?', in Conor, G. & Costas, D. (eds.), *The Cambridge Companion to Human Rights Law*, Cambridge: Cambridge University Press, pp. 329–347.

Moyn, S. (2014) *Human Rights and the Uses of History*, London: Verso.

Mullainathan, S. & Shafir, E. (2013) *Scarcity. Why Having Too Little Means So Much*, London: Penguin.

Nader, L. (1984) 'From Disputing to Complaining', in Black, D. (ed.), *Toward a General Theory of Social Control*, New York: New York Academic Press, pp. 71–94.

Nader, L. (2002) *The Life of the Law: Anthropological Projects*, Oakland: University of California Press.

Nash, K. (2009) 'Between Citizenship and Human Rights', in *Sociology*, 43: 1067–1083.

Neimanis, A. (2009) 'Bodies of Water, Human Rights and the Hydrocommons', in *Topia* 21: 161–182.

Neimanis, A. (2014) 'Natural Others? On Nature, Culture, and Knowledge', in Evans, M. et al. (eds.), *Handbook of Feminist Theories*, London: Sage Publication.

NeJaime, D. (2003) 'Marriage, Cruising, and Life in Between: Clarifying Organizational Positionalities in Pursuit of Polyvocal Gay-Based Advocacy', in *Harvard Civil Rights-Civil Liberties Law Review*, 38: 512–562.

Nussbaum, M. (2003a) 'Capabilities as Fundamental Entitlements: Sen and Social Justice', in *Feminist Economics*, 9(II–III): 33–59.

Nussbaum, M. (2003b) 'Women and Human Development', in *Mind* 112(446): 372–375.

Nussbaum, M. (2006) 'Poverty and Human Functioning: Capabilities as Fundamental Entitlements', in *Poverty and Inequality*, Standford (CA): Standford University Press, pp. 47–75.

Nussbaum, M. (2011) *Creating Capabilities*, London: Penguin.

Okin, S. M. (1989) *Justice, Gender and the Family*, New York: Basic Books.

Onnis, S. (2013) 'Dal diritto vigente alla nuda vita delle persone con disabilità intellettiva', in *Italian Journal of Disability Studies/Rivista Italiana di Studi sulla Disabilità*, 1(1): 108–132.

Pitch, T. (2013) *Contro il decoro. L'uso politico della pubblica decenza*, Roma-Bari: Laterza.
Posners, E. (2014a) *The Twilight of Human Rights Law*, Oxford and New York: Oxford University Press.
Posners, E. (2014b) 'The Case against Human Rights, *The Guardian*, 4 December, available on-line at http://www.theguardian.com/news/2014/dec/04/-sp-case-against-human-rights (last accessed October 2018).
Preciado, B. (2014) *Pornotopia: An Essay on Playboy's Architecture and Biopolitics*, Cambridge (MA) and London: MIT Press.
Ravitch, D. (2003) *The Language Police: How Pressure Groups Restrict What Students Learn*, New York: Alfred A. Knopf.
Rawls, J. (1971) *A Theory of Justice*, Cambridge (MA): Harvard University Press.
Rich, A. (1986) *Of Women Born. Motherhood as Experience and Institution*, London and New York: Norton & Company.
Schönpflug, K. (2008) *Feminism, Economics and Utopia Time Travelling through Paradigms*, Abingdon and New York: Routledge.
Secchi, B. (2013) *La città dei ricchi e la città dei poveri*, Roma-Bari: Laterza.
Secchi, B. & Viganò, P. (2009) *Antwerp: Territory of a New Modernity*, Amsterdam: Sun Publishers.
Seidman, S. (1993) *Fear of a Queer Planet: Queer Politics and Social Theory*, Minneapolis: University of Minnesota Press.
Sen, A. (1992) *Inequality Reexamined*, New York: Oxford University Press.
Sen, A. (1997) 'Economics, Business Principles and Moral Sentiments', in *Business Ethics Quarterly*, 7(3): 5–15.
Sen, A. (1999) *Development as Freedom*, New York: Oxford University Press.
Sen, A. (2010) *The Idea of Justice*, London: Penguin.
Serrano, J. (2013) *Excluded. Making Feminism and Queer Movements More Inclusive*, Berkeley (CA): Seal Press.
Shakespeare, T. (2006) *Disability Rights and Wrongs*, Abingdon: Routledge.
Sherry, M. (2004) 'Overlaps and Contradictions between Queer Theory and Disability Studies', in *Disability and Society*, 19(7): 769–783.
Snyder, S. L. & Mitchell, D. T. (2000) *Narrative Prosthesis: Disability and the Dependencies of Discourse*, Ann Arbor (MI): The University of Michigan Press.
Snyder, S. L. & Mitchell, D. T. (2006) *Cultural Location of Disability*, London: The University of Chicago Press.
Sossi, F. (2006) *Migrare. Spazi di confinamento e strategie di esistenza*, Milano: Il Saggiatore.
Spanier, B. (1995) 'Biological Determinism and Homosexuality', in *National Women's Studies Association Journal*, 7(1): 54–71.
Spanò, M. (2013) *Azioni collettive. Soggettivazione, governamentalità, neoliberismo*, Napoli: Editoriale Scientifica.
Sparti, D. (2001) 'Institutional Reflexivity or Social Control? Making up People: On Some Looping Effects of the Human Kind', in *European Journal of Social Theory*, 4(3): 331–349.
Spivak, G. C. (1988) 'Can the Subaltern Speak?', in Nelson, C. & Grossberg, L. (eds.), *Marxism and the Interpretation of Culture*, Basingstoke: Macmillan Education, pp. 271–313, available on-line at http://www.mcgill.ca/files/crclaw-discourse/Can_the_subaltern_speak.pdf (last accessed October 2018).
Stevens, B. (2011) 'Interrogating Transability: A Catalyst to View Disability as Body Art', in *Disability Study Quarterly*, 31(4), available on-line at http://dsq-sds.org/article/view/1705/1755 (last accessed October 2018).

Stiker, H. (1997) *Corps infirmes et sociétiés*, Paris: Éditions Dunod.

Stiker, R. (ed.) (1999) *History of Disability*, Ann Arbor (MI): The University of Michigan Press.

Swennen, F. & Croce, M. (2015) 'The Symbolic Power of Legal Kinship Terminology. An Analysis of 'Co-motherhood' and 'Duo-motherhood' in Belgium and the Netherlands', in *Social & Legal Studies*, published online first September 10.

UPIAS (1975) *Fundamental Principles of Disability. Being a Summary of the Discussion Held on 22nd November, 1975 and Containing Commentaries from Each Organisation*, available on-line at http://disability-studies.leeds.ac.uk/files/library/UPIAS-fundamental-principles.pdf (last accessed October 2018).

Valverde, M. (2012) *Everyday Law on the Street: City Governance in an Age of Diversity*, Chicago (IL): University of Chicago Press.

Venditti, V. (2014) 'Maternità reloaded: Una riflessione sui processi di assimilazione e normalizzazione delle forme alternative di maternità', in *Politica & Società*, 3: 449–466.

Venditti, V. (2019) 'Exponential Territorialization. Reduce, Refuse or Reuse? An Exploration of the Territories of Inclusive Legal Norms and Gender Binary', in Agha, P. (ed.), *Law, Politics and the Gender Binary*, London and New York: Routledge, pp. 21–32.

Villani, A. (2012) 'Social Justice and Capability Approach: A Note on Theses of Amartya Sen and Martha Nussbaum about the Importance of Pursuing Goals of Social Justice Through the Capability Approach', in *Rivista Internazionale di Scienze Sociali*, 120(2): 225–237.

Wagenaar, H. (2017) 'Why Prostitution Policy (Usually) Fails and What to Do about It?', in *Social Sciences* 6(2), available on-line at https://www.mdpi.com/2076-0760/6/2/43/htm (last accessed November 2018).

Walters, M. (2006), *Feminism: A Very Short Introduction*, Oxford and New York: Oxford University Press.

Warner, M. (2000) *The Trouble with Normal*, Cambridge (MA): Harvard University Press.

Wegner, P. (2002) *Imaginary Communities Utopia, the Nation, and the Spatial Histories of Modernity*, Berkeley and Los Angeles: University of California Press.

West, R. (2011) 'Tragic Rights: The Rights Critique in the Age of Obama', in *William & Mary Law Review*, 53: 713–746.

West, R. (2014) 'A Tale of Two Rights', in *Boston University Law Review*, 94: 893–912.

Wittig, M. (1975) *The Lesbian Body*, Boston (MA): Beacon Press.

Wolff, J. & De-Shalit, A. (2007) *Disadvantage*, Oxford and New York: Oxford University Press.

Wollstonecraft, M. (2004) *A Vindication of the Rights of Woman*, London: Penguin.

Young, I. M. (1990) *Justice and the Politics of Difference*, Princeton (NJ): Princeton University Press.

Young, I. M. (1997) *Intersecting Voices: Dilemmas of Gender, Political Philosophy, and Policy*, Princeton (NJ): Princeton University Press.

Young, I. M. (2000) *Inclusion and Democracy*, Oxford: Oxford University Press.

Zanichelli, M. (2013) 'Paradigmi di giustizia alla prova della disabilità', in *Rivista di Filosofia del Diritto*, 1(II): 205–225.

Žižek, S. (2005) 'Against Human Rights', in *New Left Review*, 34(4): 1–18.

Index